Accounting is the hidden architecture of ou
long it's ignored social and environmental c
a timely and practical framework for aligning ... with the public interest. It is an important contribution to building impact economies worldwide.

Elizabeth Boggs-Davidsen, CEO, GSG Impact

What an extraordinary book! *The Accounting Paradox* is an Archimedean lever that put into enough hands could move the world. Who knew? Of all the foundational elements of our societal decision-making architecture, accounting is ripe to lead us to corporate reporting that is 'true and fair' for all.

David Bonbright, Leadership Group Member,
Global Partnerships, Ashoka

This book is the course correct we need for the twenty-first century. At its core Jeremy presents a solution that is powerful and beautiful in its simplicity: all profits must be recalculated to include unaccounted for costs to people and planet. It provides analysis of how we got here and offers much needed optimism by setting out how we can all contribute to this change.

Ben Carpenter, CEO, Social Value International

Capitalism is stuck. we know that it's leading to unprecedented inequalities and climate change, but nothing seems to work. *The Accounting Paradox* is an enlightening account of the history of capitalism, coupled with extremely practical steps to get us out of the current mess. Jeremy combines his thorough research, clear diagnosis with a unique sense of humour. It is a must-read not only for accountants, but for anyone who needs a dose of realism and optimism to changing the world for better. It is the antidote we need in an increasingly bleak world. Now, I'm off to implement the solutions in the book!

Bonnie Chu, Managing Director,
The Social Investment Consultancy

A thought-provoking read giving context and insight into how business has evolved to miss the mark of true value and therefore what the purpose of business should be. As a business leader that believes we should be taking ownership of our actions and impact, it's great to read an account that shows there is a solution to be better, and the solution being one that feels like it should just be common sense and 'true and fair'.

Sam Dent, CEO, House of Hackney

This book grapples with difficult – and, for some, contentious – concepts while offering a refreshing perspective on how accounting shapes global economics. It asks: How can accounting be adapted to treat people and the planet as stakeholders, equally deserving of accountability and equitable treatment, alongside business owners? It also delivers an engaging and entertaining history of how accounting arrived at its current state – and why.

Eddie Finch, Partner, Buzzacott

Since the birth of the modern financial world over five centuries ago, accounting has defined how we measure success and make decisions – shaping the livelihoods, economies and institutions that govern our world, and our lives. Yet it has locked us into a financial lens that excludes real costs imposed on society, biodiversity and the environment. *The Accounting Paradox* by Jeremy Nicholls is an important work as it exposes this reality and shows how aligning profit with real-world impacts can transform our financial systems and bring hope for sustainable development. The book calls for a rethinking and transition of these systems, embracing a future where finance serves people, society and the planet – not the other way around. A call that cannot come soon enough and that I wish we all adhere to.

Marcos Neto, UN Assistant Secretary-General and Director of UNDP's Bureau for Policy and Programme Support

This book will be on the reading lists for my students at all levels! It shows, in a highly engaging way, how accounting has fuelled climate breakdown, inequality, and injustice and how it could be tweaked to become a force for repair. It challenges readers to see that accountants no longer do accounting, they do accountability, shaping the very foundations of our economic and social future. Both a detective story and a call to action, it invites us to imagine and build a world where accounting truly serves people and the planet.

Jennifer Rose, Senior Lecturer in Accounting and Finance,
Alliance Manchester Business School

Jeremy dares to say what many in the profession avoid: accounting has helped create our economic reality, with all its damage that entrenches inequality. At a time when climate breakdown and distrust dominate headlines, this book exposes the accounting system at the heart of the problem and shows how it can be reimagined. He outlines a practical path to an accounting system that serves people and planet, building on pathways already laid out in traditions such as Islamic accounting as well as other value-based approaches to accountability. The Accounting Paradox is essential reading for anyone serious about reforming capitalism and embedding social value into decision-making.

Ainurul Rosli, Professor, Hult International Business School,
Director Social Value Malaysia

At a time of rising populism and frustration with the economic system, it is critical to consider what went wrong and how we can reroute. Few would imagine accounting has so much to offer in this change. This book is a great guide and highlights the incredible opportunity hidden in plain sight.

Delilah Rothenberg, Co-founder and Executive Director,
Predistribution Initiative (PDI)

I have known Jeremy Nicholls for nearly two decades, and in that time, I have seen him stay steadfast in his mission to transform accounting into a tool that truly serves people and the planet. From his pioneering work in social accounting and SROI to his relentless advocacy for holding businesses accountable for their wider impact, Jeremy has been a guiding light in our field of sustainability and impact investing.

As someone who helped develop IRIS (Impact Reporting and Investment Standards) and the impact investing space, I know how difficult it is to build systems that measure what really matters. Jeremy's book, *The Accounting Paradox* shows us why mainstream accounting has fallen short and, more importantly, how we can reimagine it to reflect the true costs and contributions of our actions.

Jeremy's brilliance lies in making complex ideas accessible and urgent, while never losing sight of our shared humanity.

This book is not just about numbers, it is about justice, fairness, and the possibility of creating an economy that values well-being as much as profit. It is also a great read with great stories. I am proud to call Jeremy a colleague, a friend, and now a great writer. I cannot recommend this book highly enough.

Durreen Shahnaz, Founder and CEO,
Impact Investment Exchange (IIX)

A clever and insightful narrative, with real potential to enact change.

Helen Slinger, Executive Director, Accounting for Sustainability

I'm not an accountant but there is something for everyone in this book. It is a call to positive arms and gave me hope in a world that has started to look pretty bleak. Jeremy makes this achievable and relatively straight forward.

Emma Smith, Project Manager, Empowered Conversations, Age UK

This is a must read for anyone interested in the philosophical and practical dimensions of accounting and its role in shaping organizational and societal outcomes. The book challenges readers to reconsider assumptions that could align accounting with indigenous cultural values and long-term goals.

Hon. John Tamihere, CEO, Te Whānau O Waipareira

Current financial reporting inadequately internalizes external costs, enabling continued environmental degradation and social inequities: externalities are large in magnitude, yet not reflected in company accounts, distorting incentives and policy responses. In this context, the book has the ambition to realign accounting with long-term welfare and planetary boundaries, addressing a critical gap in contemporary governance. With rigorous methodological transparency, a detailed and practical reform agenda and explicit integration, and differentiation, from current international reform efforts, *The Accounting Paradox* has strong potential to influence scholarship and practice in sustainable accounting, ensuring maximum policy impact.

Éliane Ubalijoro CEO, CIFOR-ICRAF and
Director-General, ICRAF

The Accounting Paradox

Why accounting is damaging the world (but can help repair it)

Jeremy Nicholls

First published in Great Britain by Practical Inspiration Publishing, 2026

ISBN 9781788607131 (paperback)
9781788607124 (hardback)
9781788607155 (ebook)

EU GPSR representative: LOGOS EUROPE, 9 rue Nicolas Poussin, LA ROCHELLE 17000, France Contact@logoseurope.eu

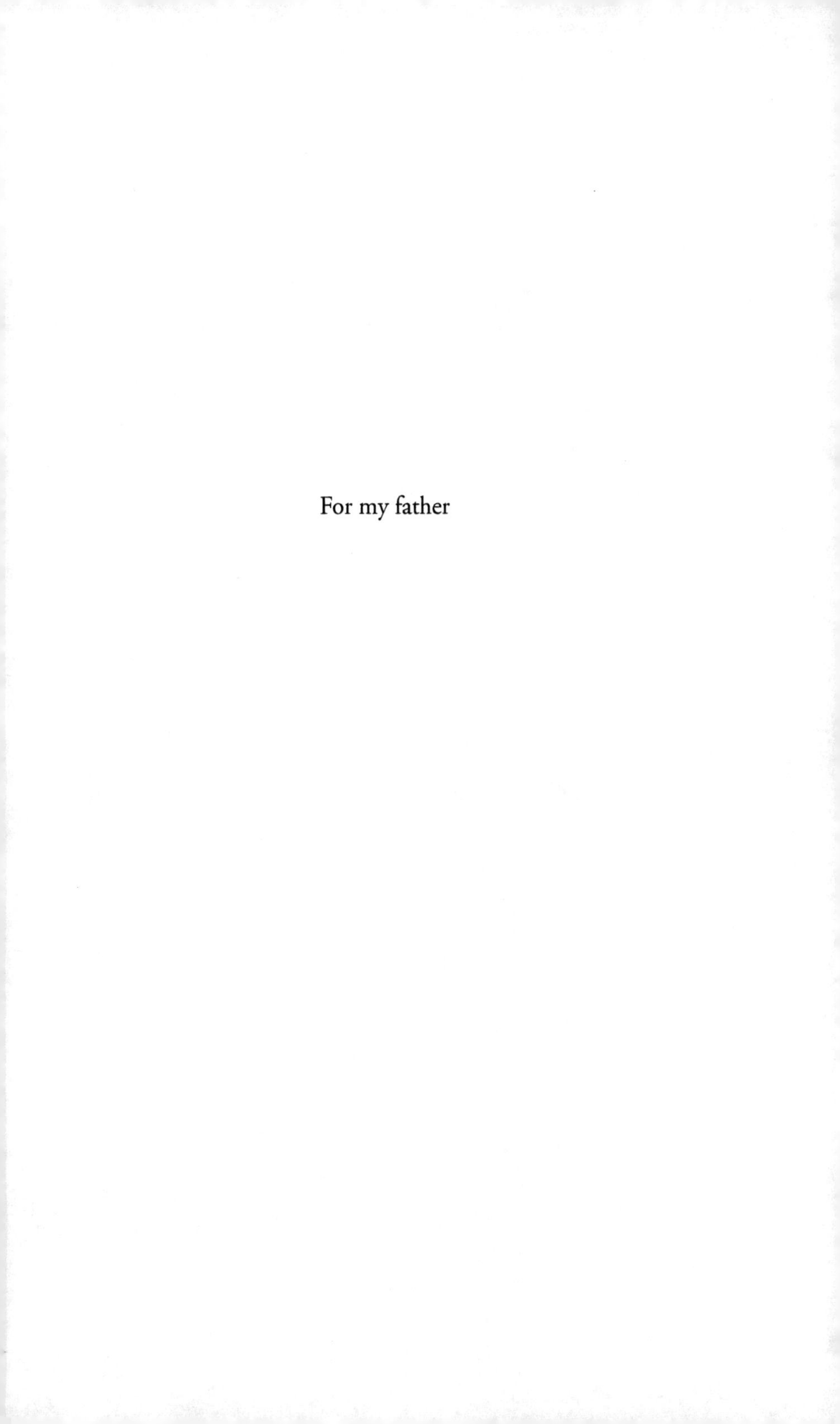

For my father

Contents

Preface

This is a book about accounting, and I am a big fan. As a student, I was also a fan of Carlos Castenada's books which explored the ways in which we construct reality. It was some time later that I read Ruth Hine's classic paper, 'Financial Accounting: In Communicating Reality, We Construct Reality', where she uses Castenada's 'Don Juan' as a metaphor for how accounting both communicates and constructs what we think of as economic reality. Accounting not only reports on the operations of a business, it is also the basis for the financial projections that inform management, lending and investment decisions. It has provided the information that has created our economy, its financial returns and its social and environmental costs. If it provided different information, we would have a different economy.

Later, as a trainee accountant coming from studying development economics, I had a nagging doubt that something wasn't right, but we had dived into double-entry book-keeping and I couldn't put my finger on the source of the doubt. I had become an accountant to go and work in Nicaragua, but this was a short-lived role as there was a change in government after I arrived. I ended up leaving accounting to become a house parent. Some time later, I returned to work, but back as an economist; I worked in regeneration and that seed of doubt slowly grew. I was one of the founders of what became an international network of people, accounting for the wider positive and negative consequences of an organization's operations, linking accounting and social cost benefit analysis. Finally, that doubt became a suspicion that mainstream accounting could, perhaps should, take these social costs, or wider consequences, into account when calculating 'profit'.

It feels as if we are living in a mash-up of every dystopic science fiction movie. If extraterrestrial life visited Earth, I suspect they might wonder why we have organized things so that so many millions live in poverty, hunger and fear in a such a rich world. A society with the knowledge and imagination to create the systems and technology we use today could surely have done better. Imagine a world where the purpose of our economy was to enable us all to live fulfilling lives and support any of us who did not, a world that was moving away from social and environmental breakdown before it is too late.

The way in which accounting practices have developed and standards have been set is amazing, coming from the experience of people across many countries, creating a way to provide useful information to make decisions about an unknown future. It is the basis for how one group of people hold another group to account for their actions. It supports local decisions, close to real time, in a disaggregated accountability system. Despite this, I now believe that accounting, specifically the purpose it is designed to achieve, is also a cause of the challenges of climate change, nature loss and social injustice.

A couple of issues will keep coming up. Externalities, where negative externalities are the negative effects of a business on people that have not been involved. Costs, and how our perception of what is or is not a cost has developed, and the accounting system, the mix accounting regulation, standards and practices.

In trying to move to something new, we must build on what we have. If we stick too closely to what we have, we may gain support but not solve the underlying problem. If we go too far, there won't be enough support for a change that is seen as too big and too hard. This is another paradox, the paradox of system change. This book is about changing our existing accounting system, enough but not too much, aligning it with expected human behaviours that are the basis for all our other social norms, and suggesting steps to make that change possible. Some of this has already started. Hopefully, by the time you read this book, more will be happening.

Glossary

AICPA	American Institute of Certified Public Accountants
CSDDD	Corporate Sustainability Due Diligence Directive
CSRD	Corporate Sustainability Reporting Directive
FAO	Food and Agriculture Organization
FCA	Financial Conduct Authority
GDP	Gross Domestic Product
GPFR	General Purpose Financial Reporting
IAASB	International Auditing and Assurance Standards Board
IAS	International Accounting Standard
IASB	International Accounting Standards Board
IASC	International Accounting Standards Committee
ICAEW	Institute of Chartered Accountants of England and Wales
ICAS	Institute of Chartered Accountants of Scotland
IESBA	International Ethics Standards Board for Accountants
IFAC	International Federation of Accountants
IFEA	International Foundation for Ethics and Audit
IMF	International Monetary Fund
IOSCO	International Organization of Securities Commissions
ISO	International Organization for Standardization
ISSA	International Standard on Sustainability Assurance
ISSB	International Sustainability Standards Board
LSE	London School of Economics
OECD	Organisation for Economic Co-operation and Development
PIOB	Public Interest Oversight Board
PSC	Public Sector Committee
SDG	Sustainable Development Goal
SEEA	System of Environmental-Economic Accounting
SNA	System of National Accounts
TCFD	Task Force on Climate-related Financial Disclosures

TISFD	Task Force on Inequality and Social-related Financial Disclosures
TNFD	Task Force on Nature-related Financial Disclosures
UNDESA	United Nations Department of Economic and Social Affairs
UNDP	United Nations Development Programme
UNEP	United Nations Environment Programme
WHO	World Health Organization

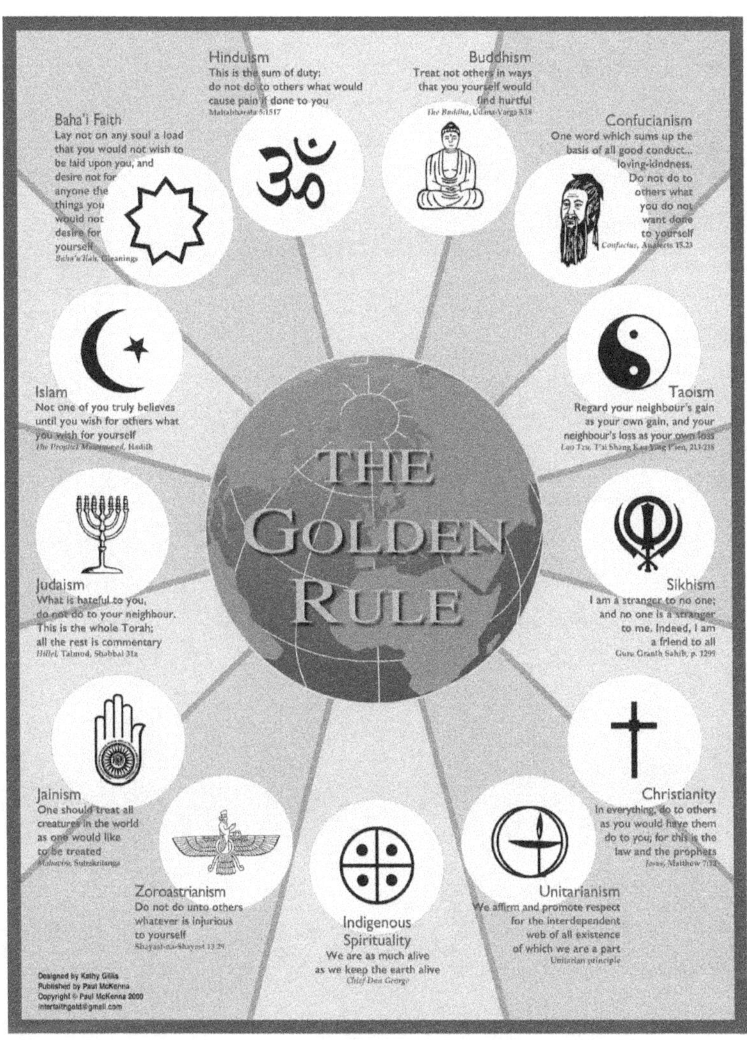

The Golden Rule

Source: Paul Mckenna at interfaithgold@gmail.com;
www.scarboromissions.ca/golden-rule/the-golden-rule-poster-a-history

Part 1

The problem: Why accounting is damaging society

On 1 June 2009, Air France 447 stalled on a flight from Rio de Janeiro to Paris, killing all passengers and crew. The primary cause was the external environment. But black box recordings suggest it was the crew's inability to understand and resolve the problem that led to a loss of control. One of the pilots continued to pull back on the side stick in an attempt to climb – the opposite of what was needed to recover.[1] By the time anyone realized what was happening, it was too late.

Climate change, nature loss and wealth inequality are bringing us all down but working people and families on lower incomes are experiencing the worst consequences. Responses to these global crises are becoming more nationalistic, while hard fought for rights are being undermined. The proposed solutions to our current collective problems, of whatever political hue, ignore accounting. Like the pilots in Air France 447 everyone is promoting or trying solutions but missing the one thing that needs to change first. There are those who argue that the problem is capitalism and this needs to be replaced with some alternative system. There are those who think that it is the excesses of capitalism that are to blame and that we only need to create a 'responsible' capitalism and all will be well. Yet others argue that capitalism is the solution, if only markets were allowed to run truly free. It's easy to conclude that it is all too hard and that there is nothing we can do. It can feel like we are all just passengers on a doomed airliner.

We seem to have moved from feudalism to capitalism, and back to feudalism again. Feudal lords at least recognized some responsibilities for their serfs but the uber rich of the twenty-first century have few legal responsibilities to the people who suffer the consequences of their wealth. It's like the Middle Ages, but with the internet and barrel bombs. There is a tendency to blame capitalism but what we call 'capitalism' is really only the behaviours that follow a break down in society's ability to hold people to account, and is not to be confused with a competitive market economy. The way in which we produce things, to meet (some) people's needs, has allowed a new group of people to gain (some) control over resources and then benefit from any financial returns from investing those resources. Until recently, accounting has served this group well.

An International Monetary Fund (IMF) working paper estimated fossil fuel subsidies in 2022 at US$7 trillion, of which 82% was undercharging for environmental costs and forgone consumption taxes.[2] In 2024, S&P Global, a leading credit ratings, benchmarks and analytics provider, assessed the environmental negative externalities generated by 12,000 companies, representing most of the market capitalization of globally public listed companies, at US$3.7 trillion[3] in 2021 alone. 26% of those companies created negative externalities that were more than their net income. This estimate did not include negative social externalities in public markets, or negative externalities in private markets or public non-traded investments, so the total annual cost would be much higher.[4] These costs are not included in companies' accounts but are still imposed on the planet and the people that live on it. It is going to take a very long time if we wait for those experiencing these costs to seek compensation through the legal system.

The fundamental problem is that companies are making and distributing profits but not taking costs into account that are imposed on other people and the planet. If we continue to account for profit in this way, we will continue to allocate resources to activities that undermine society, biodiversity and the environment, in a spiral of crisis and conflict. There is something we can do about this, something that is not actually that hard, but we have missed the fundamental cause of the problem. This is to change the way in which the system of financial accounting, a mix of regulation, standard setting and accounting practice, recognizes costs.

As an accountant, I spent far more time preparing forecasts than preparing accounts. If the accounts included these missing costs, it may not have a big effect that year, but forecasts would now have to include these costs. Some business plans would not be profitable or would have changed before anyone decided to lend to or invest in the business. Of course, other consequences may appear later, but the feedback loop would be much quicker and the rate at which new technologies are brought to the market might be a little slower. Investment flows would move away from activities that contributed to these costs. Accounting standards may be about historical information, but their power is over the decisions businesses make about future expected cashflows.

Some things turn out to do more bad than good. It must seem bizarre that business just carries on regardless of when this is the case. Links between smoking and cancer emerged as early as the 1950s[5] and the industry knew.[6] Meanwhile in 1965, the American Petroleum Institute (API) – the main US oil lobby group – released a report[7] acknowledging that CO_2 from fossil fuels could cause 'significant changes in climate'. As for asbestos, the first concern was raised by a doctor in Vienna in 1897.[8] Had the accounting system required these health and related costs to be recognized, we'd have all known a lot sooner. And many lives would have been saved.

Do unto others as you would have done unto yourself

No one really likes it when someone holds us to account and yet we all have an intrinsic sense of what is right. We know in our hearts that we should be held to account for our actions. Well perhaps not everyone, but most of us. The idea that we should do unto others as we would do unto ourselves has a long history. The UN Declaration of Human Rights was adopted in 1948 and the first article states that we should act towards one another in a spirit of brotherhood, an idea that is ancient and across cultures and became known as the Golden Rule.[9] In 1993, the Parliament of the World's Religions signed a *Declaration Toward a Global Ethic* referring to the principle as a core shared value, stating, 'We must treat others as we wish others to treat us. We make this declaration in the belief that it will help ensure a better global order.'[10] A mosaic version of Norman Rockwell's painting of the Golden Rule now hangs in the United Nations. This is not just a religious perspective, it is also an ancient spiritual and cultural perspective, fundamental to the worldviews of most Indigenous cultures who believe in the interconnectedness of people with each other and the Earth.[11] According to this view, what we do to others we also do to ourselves, for example, as reflected in the Māori principle of manaakitanga, of showing respect, generosity and care for others.[12] These perspectives can show us a way forward for our accounting system.

The problem and a solution

One of the paradoxes of 'accounting', using that term now as shorthand for the wider accounting system, is that it is the problem, but it is also the solution. Accounting and auditing are amazing and, together, they have allowed us to invest in businesses where we will never know the managers and yet we can trust them with our money. They provide us with information about uncertain futures, with uncertain returns. This equips us to make decisions with a reasonable degree of confidence, despite such uncertainties. It works because there are clear standards for financial reporting and auditing and for the competence of those applying those standards, overseen and reviewed by governments, or bodies acting under the remit of governments.

The premise that accounting is damaging the world may seem surprising, perhaps implausible. I hope that by the time you finish this book, you will be persuaded or, at least, will have a new perspective on something most of us take for granted, and only think about when we fill in an expense claim or send in a tax return. On the off-chance you think accounting is boring, I hope to persuade you otherwise. Throughout the book, the issues are framed by five questions that Tony Benn, a member of UK parliament until 2001, asked about power and accountability. 'What power have you got? Where did you get it from? In whose interests do you use it? To whom are you accountable? How do we get rid of you?'

This book is a detective story – of sorts. And a manifesto for change. It ends with practical steps we can take to balance the speed of change we need with the economic system's ability to handle change, broken up against the different roles we all have. You may be an accountant, a lawyer, a company director or an investor, or you may simply work in a business that produces accounts. If you have a pension, you are an investor. But you may also be a citizen, or an activist or a student – and you may know a director. Together, we can fix the problem.

Chapter 1

Financial accounting and the mess we are in

Are we really in a mess?

From one perspective, the world has been getting richer, so it may seem to some that problems are overstated and accounting is doing just fine. It is always easy to list all the terrible things going on and to lose sight of how much has changed – and changed for the better. Leaving aside the challenges with using Gross Domestic Product (GDP) as a measure of progress,[1] on the face of it living standards been rising for years. Surely this is all good. The graph[2] that follows shows just how good. But not so good if the benefits are spread unevenly. There are around 650 million people living in absolute poverty, surviving on less than US$2.15[3] per day, and there are 2.8 billion people now living on less than US$6.85 a day.

That increase in GDP growth over the last 200 years is, of course, very impressive. But it also highlights the possible scale and increase in the costs that the accounting system has allowed us to exclude from the calculation of profit, that led to the increase in GDP. The increase has been driven by using the planet's limited resources and by abusing people's human rights. It results from government's ability to borrow against future generations' desire and ability to pay our debts and because choosing investments based on the present value of future cashflows undervalues cashflows for future generations. Because of all these missing costs, we have not efficiently priced the use of the resources on which both current and future generations depend.

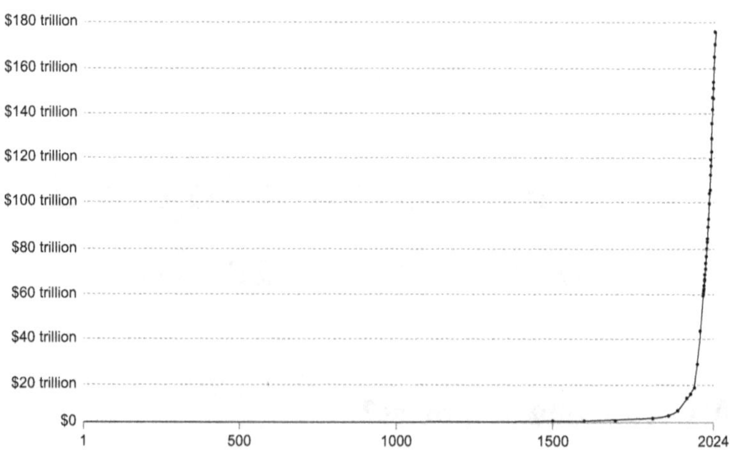

Figure 1.1: Global GDP over the long run

Source: Our World in Data. "Global GDP over the long run." Based on data from Eurostat, OECD, World Bank (2025); Maddison Project Database (2023). Adapted under CC BY 4.0. Available at: https://ourworldindata.org/economic-growth. Adapted from original. Modifications include removal of footer notes and branding.

Industrialization and the use of fossil fuels has also played a big role in the growth in GDP. But that is only half the story. Colonialism and enslaving people made a significant contribution, and the increase was accompanied by a shift in the distribution of GDP around the world. In the seventeenth century, distribution of GDP was broadly even across Africa, Asia, Europe, North and South America.[4] In 2024, North America, Europe and East Asia (with a combined GDP of nearly US$90tn) together made up nearly 80% of the world's GDP in nominal terms.[5] These parts of the world managed to increase their GDP much more than everywhere else. And using percentages can hide underlying changes, for example, the percentage of people in poverty can go down while the absolute number in poverty goes up.

The global economic system supports the investments and returns that underpin the growth in GDP. This complex system is reasonably effective at holding businesses, and the people who use that capital, accountable for their performance in creating financial returns and is not really designed to do anything else. The system's mix of laws, standards and a good dose of politics is the basis for a competitive market economy and the way in which accounting measures financial returns lies at its heart. Good performance against this measure attracts more investment, poor performance results in people losing their jobs and businesses closing. We measure this performance against profit or loss.

Life expectancy has jumped. Eleventh-century life expectancy at birth was around 30 years and around 50 for those who survived their first five years.[6] Now it is over 70 years at birth,[7] more than double.[8] The big change has been in increasing life expectancy for the under-fives, which increased from 50% in the eleventh century to 96% in 2023,[9] a massive and relatively recent rise. Most of the increase has been since the end of the nineteenth century with antibiotics and improvements in public health and maternity care.[10] GDP growth and life expectancy are related but increases in life expectancy tail off as incomes increase. The life expectancy of people in extreme poverty is lower. It is difficult to know how much lower but, in the UK, the gap in life expectancy between people on highest and lowest incomes is around 10 years.[11] In the eleventh century nearly everyone was in extreme poverty, so the average life expectancy of everyone was still around 30. According to the World Population Review[12] in 2024, the lowest average life expectancy, by country, is in the 50s which is still a big increase.

It is hard to estimate the world population in the eleventh century, perhaps about 350 million.[13] By the nineteenth century it was around 1 billion and it is now over 8 billion.[14] In 2018, there were around 650 million people in extreme poverty,[15] double the number in the eleventh century, though this number has come down as both a proportion and, since the nineteenth century, also in absolute numbers, as shown in Figure 1.2 below. Recent research suggests that existing methods of measuring how many people there are in the world have underestimated rural populations by as much as half.[16] If true, the number of people in extreme poverty could be much higher.

Are things better now than in the eleventh century? Of course, especially for the under-fives. Yes, in terms of life expectancy. In terms of absolute numbers and in terms of healthy lives, it depends

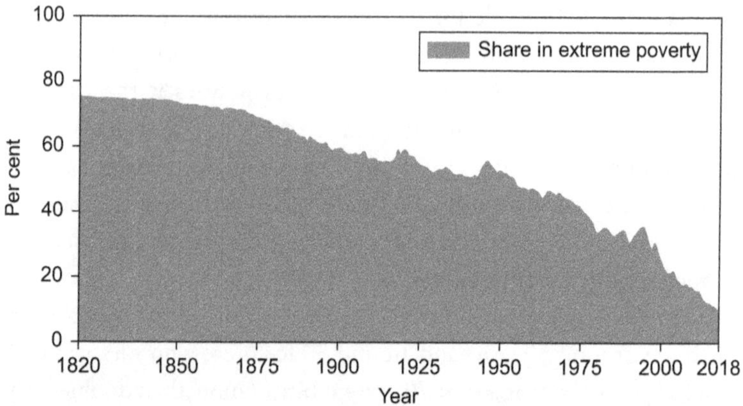

Figure 1.2: Share of world population living in extreme poverty

Source: Michalis Moatsos (2021), via *Our World in Data.* 'Share of population living in extreme poverty, World.' Adapted from original at OurWorldInData.org/extreme-poverty-in-brief. Licensed under CC BY 4.0.

where you start from, and we have had 800 years since the eleventh century to get this right and a huge increase in global GDP to pay for it. So not quite as impressive as it might look at first sight. And it may be a high point. We really could and should have done a lot better.

In a market economy as some people gain rights over resources, they provide resources (investments) to support the provision of goods and services and then require a payment for the use of those resources (financial returns). The goods and services are provided by groups of people working together in a complex mix of contractual and legal arrangements that we call businesses or enterprises, and these businesses need a way to measure whether they can continue to provide these goods and services over time, allowing investors to move resources to those that are making profits most efficiently and effectively and every day new businesses start and old businesses close. Accounting knits all this together. The accounting system is more than a process of recording information, it is a system made up of regulation, standards, and accounting and auditing practice which come together to determine what information is required, how it should be prepared and how and when it can be safely used.

But it is also about power. Those with power define and control knowledge, and the accounting system is a perfect example of how those with power have defined, and controlled, what gets accounted for. It is perfect because the use of power is concealed. The system creates unquestionable norms and separates consequences from causes. It has intensified and concealed exploitation, recording as 'knowledge' the extraction of value as much as the creation of value. By deciding which costs to account for it has also decided which costs can be excluded. The resulting reports, financial statements, inform decisions that result in both profits for some and costs for others. Whether we call these 'not accounted for' costs, not 'held to account for' costs, 'hidden' costs, 'losses of well-being' costs or 'negative externalities' (and all these descriptions and others will be used to find one that lands most effectively) the cause and effect will be the same.

Whatever people may say, we are not very good at holding ourselves to account, people do not make decisions that are against their own interests. Effective accountability requires someone else to hold us to account, and in business, to hold directors to account. Customers, investors, auditors and regulators all have a role to play in deciding what they are held to account for and making sure the approach taken is effective.

For most of us accounting just counts money – how much money a business has, owes, or is owed. The paradox is that accounting contributes to helping businesses create value, but by excluding costs arising from a business's impacts on others and dependencies on resources that were not paid for, it also extracts value.

What are costs?

Whether or not a business is accountable for costs and should include them in the accounts will determine the price at which goods or services are sold, the level of demand and the expected and actual profit. So, the question of which costs are included is critical. This is not a discussion about business or social costs, it is discussion about how society has normalized the difference.

Accounting isn't neutral. Intrinsically, it is a list and includes costs in the list. The critical questions are what gets in the list, who decides and who checks the list is complete. A cost is not the same as paying for something. If someone experiences a loss, for example a loss of income, that is still a cost, whether or not a business caused it or whether the business has to pay for that loss. The loss could also be having less of something that you have sold to the business and been paid for. This may seem a strange way of looking at the question of cost, but it is important to separate the loss, or the reduction, from the payment. The first question is then is the business responsible, the second is will it have to pay. Accounting tends to conflate these by describing a liability which is the amount the business is liable for and will pay. There is a liability if there is a legal or constructive obligation which a business cannot avoid paying. If there is no legal or constructive obligation, there is no expected payment and so no cost. The risk is that losses, or costs, are imposed by the business on other people, but it can avoid paying for these costs because there is no obligation.

The challenge will be showing causality between a business's actions and the consequential loss. The easiest solution is when those involved agree the consequences of an action in advance. Accounting has primarily focused on transactions between a business and its customers, suppliers and investors; transactions where those involved have agreed to what is expected and probably documented expectations in a formal contract. Other legally enforceable obligations, for example taxes or fines, are also included. And fines are ways of making a business responsible for costs it might otherwise avoid.

Legally enforceable costs are not the only source of costs. What if I suffer damages while you are delivering a contract for a third party? I have my car in the garage, and it gets damaged while the mechanic is working on another car. I'd expect the garage to pay for the damage and, if I hadn't been paid by the time the annual accounts are prepared, I might expect to see the cost in the garage's accounts. Of course, the garage might claim the damage was there when I brought the car in, and so it starts to get complicated. Will I try and enforce payment? If I go to court, will I win? For accountants, these 'Will a payment need to be made?' situations that might create a contingent liability. The liability to pay that is contingent on a future event, in this example, the outcome of a legal process that would make the cost enforceable. The more probable the outcome is that the garage must pay, the more likely that the cost will have to be included in the accounts.

Where those not directly involved in a transaction did not agree, it becomes possible to argue about existence of any costs and then whether or to what extent the business caused them. One thing is clear, the less costs you pay, the more profit you can make. The incentive is to limit costs to those that are legally enforceable. Joseph Heath,[17] in defining profit, said: 'It is best therefore to think of profit as what is left over after all the firm's contractual obligations have been met.' And that might seem obvious to most of us, but accounting standards do provide for some costs that were not agreed in advance but only if it is reasonably likely that the business will have to pay.

Even where the link between an action and a cost can be made, whether or not a business will have to pay depends on if the people, or a public authority, experiencing the loss, are able to take the business to court and win. It isn't easy to find the total amount that BP paid out following the 2010 Deepwater Horizon Oil Spill, but it was billions of dollars. And at one point the company had set aside US$43 billion to cover fines and other legal costs.[18] And it wasn't just BP. The courts had to decide on the share of responsibility between BP, Transocean and Halliburton, with BP shouldering most of the responsibility. The courts also had to decide how far to go in determining an obligation to compensation and the amount to be paid to those who could show a drop in income caused by the disaster. This included people whose income was directly affected, like fishermen, but also businesses that depended on their business. There were many side effects to consider, including psychological, physical, economic, sociological and cultural impacts.[19] The court's decision determines which of these costs become legally enforceable and will be accounted for.

This is hard enough in high profile cases, especially where the loss is experienced by many people who must come together and mount a 'class action'. There are other examples – for example, Birmingham City Council's settlement of 6,000 claims from current and past employees for equal pay.[20] The court determined the costs that Birmingham City Council will pay and which will now be included in their accounts. These are high profile examples that made it to court. Imagine how hard this will be when the loss is experienced by only one or two people, who do not have the resources to take a company to court and win their case, let alone be able to force payment. It must surely be that for most instances of a business causing indirect damage to others, the costs are neither recognized nor paid.

If Birmingham City Council had won the case and not had to pay, the cost was still being imposed. The women have still been paid less than the men. Equally just because a business does not pay for the cost of using carbon, the harm done to people and the planet is still a cost. Shareholders, and that includes any of us with a pension, may not worry about which costs were included and how our returns were earned, assuming that international accounting and auditing standards will give us comfort. Cold comfort though, I'm afraid. If the purpose of accounting is to provide users with information to make decisions based on the expectation of financial returns, users are assumed to have no expectations of, or interest in, what happens to other people. The system is designed as if users have no empathy, no guilt and no remorse if others are harmed or mistreated.

Excluded costs

If costs are not in the financial accounts, they won't be in calculations of GDP, but they still exist. There are costs missing from every single trade, every single day. Some are small, some are large. No one knows what the real price would be if they were included. If they were included, some transactions would still go ahead. Some wouldn't. Relative prices would change throughout the year. New products and services with new prices would be introduced and relative prices would change again. That's how business works. And you might think, at this point, that this is all very well, but we can't calculate these other costs. We cannot measure, value or allocate them to a particular business, let alone each individual transaction. But as we shall see, we can.

Costs imposed on other people, or the planet, go much further than costs arising from environmental disasters and low and unequal pay. They include household labour costs; where businesses depend on someone somewhere providing their services for free, or creating and fly-tipping greenhouse gas emissions into the atmosphere for free. Costs imposed by the effects of climate change on your life. Costs imposed when you are forced to take on several jobs all paid below a living wage. Costs from not being paid at all. Costs imposed on lower income people and households and on women more than on men.[21] It might be tempting to call some costs business costs and others societal costs or something similar. This would be to reinforce and accept an approach which has become a norm, one that allows businesses to exclude the cost of some resources used and harm done because these are somehow out of scope. As Paul Polman pointed out: 'In these stores, if you break something, you own it, you pay for it. That is how most stores work. Why does that not work with business? If you break it, you own it.'[22]

Excluded costs have been piling up, but someone else is still paying, and the company imposing them has no incentive to reduce them. Over the last few years, these costs have become obvious, even if we have missed accounting's role. The scale of these costs means we might finally have a chance to realize what accounting has been doing. A clue as to the scale is the growing calls for reparations. Reparations are not new, for example the Allied Powers required Germany to pay reparations after World War I. They may not be the first thing you think of in connection with accounting. But one consequence of allowing business to make profits which exclude costs will be when they pile up so high that they become claims for reparations.

In 2021, NBC News asked Olivia Grange, Jamaica's Minister of Culture, Gender, Entertainment and Sport, if global powers would finally listen to the calls for reparations for historical slavery.[23] Her reply was: 'Our African ancestors were forcibly removed from their home and suffered unparalleled atrocities to carry out forced labour to the benefit of the British Empire. Redress is well overdue.' It's easy, or perhaps convenient, to forget just how much our global economic system is dependent on colonialism. The resources (often taken, rarely paid for, in what would be recognized as a free market) helped establish the financial institutions on which the economic system now depends.

Whatever the pros and cons of the arguments for reparation, or the ability of governments to pay, there is another point here. These costs will go on piling up. Systemic abuses of people's human rights continue, and our global economy continues to depend on unpaid and underpaid labour. Even in wealthy countries, gender pay inequality persists.[24] Until and unless we change accounting, we will go on allowing businesses to account for profits and pay out dividends to some that exclude costs for many others. The damage is accumulating, all the time, every day. Accounting may set out to measure the profit businesses create but it is also a way of hiding the value investors extract.

Uncertainty

Financial statements provide information to users making decisions in the expectation of financial returns. For the information to be useful it must be relevant to those decisions and it must reach a level of certainty that is implicit in the risk users are willing to accept in making those decisions. These decisions depend on an assessment of likely future cashflows, which means that all the items in those financial statements relate back to future cashflows – which are uncertain. There is even uncertainty in the money reported in the bank. If a bank account is in a different currency to the currency used for reporting, there will be exchange rate uncertainty. And perhaps there was another bank account you forgot about. The one with the large overdraft.

There are three types of uncertainty in accounting: existence, outcome and measurement. Think about a debt that a company is owed. There may be uncertainty as to whether a debt exists, if the person we claim owes us the money disputes the debt. There may be uncertainty about whether we will recover all or only some of the debt. Or the contract may have included clauses that make the final payment uncertain. At some point the uncertainty becomes so high that the debt cannot be included in the profit and loss account and is moved to the notes to the accounts. If it becomes so uncertain that the information would mislead users, it would not be included at all. I had the experience early in my short audit career, auditing a building company that had accounted for the share of the profit it would make from contracts that would take several years to fulfil. The uncertainty over those contracts, and whether in fact there would be any profit, meant we did not accept the company's accounts, leading to meetings between the audit partner and the directors well above my pay grade.

Accounting standards do not define a level of acceptable uncertainty in numeric terms, but it deals with this in ways that are both pragmatic and effective. Financial accounting's approach to uncertainty is the result of years of practice in producing information and then putting in checks and balances so that it is good enough for users. Defining the users and the purpose is only the start; accounting then defines the information and the types of uncertainty. Third-party audit of the result is critical to address the risk of 'material misstatement' (accounting speak for the risk of an error that matters to users). The audit partner assesses the audit risk; the risk that the audit may not identify missing information that matters (or information that has been included that does not matter and obscures the rest). The audit work should bring this risk down to an acceptable level, within the context of a level of uncertainty that accounting cannot calculate, but is a general level of uncertainty, common to the risk those primary users are willing to accept in using information. This is all excellent. This general level will not be the same for everyone. Many lawsuits arise when someone buys a company and discovers all sorts of costs that were not in the accounts. Should the accounts have included them or were they legitimately not certain enough?

Unaccounted costs mean value is being extracted

There is growing recognition that investments are contributing to costs that are not included, though imposed on others, *even though they are generating financial returns*. This has resulted in a boom in the number of networks, organizations and standards including specific initiatives to allocate costs back to business such as 'the polluter pays'. But changes to financial accounting and how profit is calculated have not been on the table. Accounting is seen as inviolate, just a neutral technique. It is the servant, not the master, and has no role to play as either part of the problem or part of the solution. After all, most of us might think that financial accounting is just an account of the money we have received and the money we pay out and what is left is our profit. Profit that can be returned to the people who provided the money. Financial returns are just that: a return on finance, a dividend. Exciting stuff.

One consequence is that we then create a culture that supports all this. It is not that directors and managers have hidden these costs, they have no incentive to manage them. Whatever the truth, it would not be surprising that they have little interest in the consequences for others if their performance is only measured against financial returns.

The former President of Zaire, Mobutu Sese Seko, said, 'Everything is for sale, anything can be bought in our country. And in this flow, he who holds the slightest cover of public authority uses it illegally to acquire money, goods, prestige or to avoid obligations.'[25] Mobuto's concerns were more about corruption in his country, but the accounting system has provided the very same cover of public authority to allow investors to acquire money, goods, prestige and avoid obligations – and, worse still, it is legal.

If you have power, you can control and define knowledge. and create institutions to protect your power. The accounting system controls what costs to include in the calculation of profit. Far from mediating against human excesses, it encourages them. And yet who would notice? We accept it without a second thought. The result is that externalities are going through the roof. Hard to know how far and how much, given no one accounts for them, but probably very similar to the trend in GDP in the graph earlier.

When Alan Jope stepped down as CEO of Unilever, one of the investors, Terry Smith, said 'A company which feels it has to define the purpose of Hellmann's mayonnaise has in our view clearly lost the plot.'[26] As if a purpose of making mayonnaise without doing any harm to anyone was unnecessary. If all business decisions took these other costs into account, decision makers might be more risk averse, a bit more deliberative, even empathetic. And do more to include others in their success.

Although later chapters will deal with what taking these costs into account might look like in practice, it is probably important to say, early on, that accounting for externalities does not mean accounting for every single one. The solution will not be to go from an accounting system based on judgement to one based on an absolutist view. There will still be judgement, and the accounting system is brilliantly placed to move the boundary at which we account for costs to a new but better place. It is in that liminal space that the magic will happen.

Chapter 2

How have we managed to miss this?

Price is not always a good measure of value. The extent to which people still talk about high value jobs for highly paid people, when Covid-19 has shown us that it is the relatively low paid jobs that are high value, shows just how much worth and price have become false substitutes.

In his Reith Lectures, 'How We Get What We Value',[1] Mark Carney, a former Governor of the Bank of England and currently the Prime Minister of Canada, explored the question of value, the challenges we face and solutions to the climate crisis. He asked why many of the resources on which our businesses depend are not in a ledger and gave the example of the Amazon rainforest only appearing when it has become a cattle farm.

Carney argued that markets are the cause of the substitution of price for worth and have run away with themselves. The most common solution to market failure (more markets and less regulation) only makes the problems worse. He also recognized that society's goal is to increase well-being – a way to ensure that society's values drive the creation of economic value. So far, so good. But perhaps extraordinarily for a banker, he made no mention of financial accounting as part of the solution beyond the early comment about a ledger. And yet there would be no banking without accounting, a very different economics without accounting and no investment driving growth of any kind, carbon neutral or not, without accounting. It was as if accounting was completely neutral and so we can ignore it.

Economics and accounting

Economists know that a market economy can give rise to other costs and benefits. They call them externalities, and negative externalities are another way of describing harm done to others. These all affect the allocation of resources to activities and what products and services are available in a market economy. After all, '[e]xternalities occur when producing or consuming a good, causes an impact on third parties not directly related to the transaction'.[2] There is extensive theory and practice on how these costs and benefits can be internalized.

The economist, Ronald Coase[3] argued that externalities also occur if people who are party to production or consumption, experience costs that are not paid because there are transaction costs and unequal negotiating power. When someone has no alternative, perhaps they do not have time to explore other options, and accepts a job paying below the living wage, they will be experiencing a cost, as they are not earning enough on which to live. This is also an externality. And we have a market that leads to inefficient resource allocation where there is a difference between private returns (investor) and societal returns (an underpaid person who needs enough to live).

We know that externalities are a bad thing because there is then a difference between private returns and societal returns, which means resource allocation is inefficient. The International Monetary Fund (IMF),[4] in a 'Back-to-Basics' article, points out that:

> To promote the well-being of all members of society, social returns should be maximized and social costs minimized. This implies that all costs and benefits need to be internalized by households and firms making buying and production decisions. Otherwise, market outcomes involve underproduction of goods or services that entail positive externalities or overproduction in the case of negative externalities.

Overproduction of goods with negative externalities pretty much sums up the climate crisis. Many of the global challenges we face from climate change, nature loss and inequality result from businesses' negative impacts or their dependency on using resources which are either not costed or are under-costed. In other words, externalities. Economists have focused on addressing the problem through government action, rather than going back to the root cause. As the same IMF paper says,

> Consumption, production, and investment decisions of individuals, households, and firms often affect people not directly involved in the transactions. Sometimes these indirect effects are tiny. But when they are large, they can become problematic – what economists call externalities. Externalities are among the main reasons governments intervene in the economic sphere.

Sometimes they are tiny, sometimes they are large. But how large is large? And what about direct? If it's indirect, is it no longer an externality, even though it is still a cost someone is experiencing, that a business has not included in the cost of production? In *The Road to Freedom*, Stiglitz devotes a chapter to the issue reminding us that, 'Externalities are everywhere… Key questions of economic policy entail managing externalities.'

According to Investopedia,[5] the difference between accounting and economics is that 'Accountants track the flow of money for businesses and individuals. Economists track the larger trends that drive money and the resources that money represents. Both help businesses and governments plan, make sound financial decisions, and set fiscal policies.'

Any microeconomics course has a theory of the firm, which shows the demand for a firm's products and, what it can supply, at different prices. But costs are in input to price, and, in practice, accounting decides which costs are an input. Economists have developed a range of solutions to internalizing externalities, but appear to have missed one option, changing how the accountancy system recognizes costs.

The problem arises when deciding what a business needs, to be able to supply something in a market. A simple answer would be the inputs that you have to pay for – for example, employees, raw materials, plant and machinery. You'll know how much all this costs because you have contracts, and the person selling you something will have worked out their own costs in agreeing to contract with you. Then there will be other legally enforceable obligations as well, for example taxes, levies, fines and pension contributions. This may seem so obvious that it doesn't need consideration. But it would be an assumption to say that accountancy could not include non-legally enforceable obligations. Earlier, in Chapter 1 (What are costs?), obligations were defined as legal or constructive and accounting standards allow for constructive obligations. From the perspective of an investment manager looking to make financial returns for their clients, leaving these obligations out might look good. From the perspective of society, allocating scarce resources to competing demands, it is proving an unmitigated disaster.

As Adam Smith put it,

> Every individual… neither intends to promote the public interest, nor knows how much he is promoting it… he intends only his own security; and by directing that industry in such a manner as its produce may be of the greatest value, he intends only his own gain, and he is in this, as in many other cases, led by an invisible hand to promote an end which was no part of his intention.[6]

Smith's 'invisible hand' is invisible because the link to an end wasn't clear, but the link is accounting. Far from reining in humanities worst characteristics, the current application of accounting standards actively encourages them. Accounting is, literally, the standards bearer for capitalism and the invisible hand.

The early economists – Smith, Ricardo and Marx – understandably paid little attention to the role of accounting, even as Marx explored surplus labour value. There was little legislation or regulation and no standards for accounting. But the consequences, if not one of the causes, of missing costs out were already being recognized and, in some cases, fought for: decent wages, overtime, holidays, equal pay and sick pay. Critical accounting argues that accounting shapes reality and this includes how costs are recognized[7] and there is a risk to economic theory and practice if this is missed. Doughnut Economics' guidance for businesses[8] includes a reference, in the governance section, to the annual accounts which does gets close, stating, 'The governance structure of a business determines how decisions are made. This covers who is represented on the board, how trade-offs are navigated, transparency of the business, what information and metrics are included in annual accounts'.

In the eleventh century the average number of direct transactions a person might make in a year was small, perhaps under 100. Roll forward to now and it is thousands, in a mix of digital payments, online shopping and subscriptions. According to McKinsey's 2024 global payments report,[9] in 2023 the global payments industry alone handled 3.4 trillion transactions, an average of around 400 per person. Add indirect transactions through more complex supply chains, and it is even more. Many are small but each transaction comes with the potential to contribute to externalities. It should be easy to see how lots of small negative externalities can add up to very big problems, yet government interventions are often slow off the mark, may not intervene where necessary, or may choose interventions that have unintended side effects.

We should stop saying 'negative externalities' or 'sustainability issues' and call these things out: they are harm done to the people and planet or, for short, 'harm done'.

GDP is just more interesting

Meanwhile, our economic system has blithely assumed that growth means more wealth for future generations, that this wealth will allow governments to reduce their national debts. Until, that is, population growth slows, or the benefits are concentrated, and there are not enough people able to spend with enough income to keep the show on the road.

As US presidential candidate Robert Kennedy put it in his 1968 election speech,[10] 'it [GDP] measures everything, except that which makes life worthwhile'. The argument that GDP is a flawed way of measuring changes in a society's well-being has gained ground. As an example of what GDP misses, if I pay you to provide childcare for my children and you pay me to provide childcare for your children, we are adding to GDP. If we look after our own children, we do not. No economic transaction, no GDP effect. Not that we have stopped using GDP, but something is clearly not working if GDP is rising at the same time as climate change is bringing us to the edge of meltdown. The main criticisms are that it misses things that contribute to the well-being of people and society, including unpaid household work and enjoyment of nature and that it is not a good way to measure progress. What we need is a way to measure quality of life and well-being.

Those responsible for calculating GDP point out that they do not intend it to be a measure of well-being. Fair enough. GDP is a measure of economic activity that relates to financial transactions between households, organizations and government. Unfortunately, in the absence of anything else, people use it as a proxy for social well-being. GDP up = good; GDP down = bad. Even if true, why do we measure economic activity? The UK's Office for National Statistics' own explanation[11] states that 'GDP is the standard measure of the size and health of a country's economy. It's the way we measure and compare how well or badly countries are doing.' What is the point of a healthy economy if not to create value for the people that live in that economy?

So, we use economic activity as a proxy for well-being.[12] If the point of measurement is to inform decisions to increase well-being and we are using information that is both a proxy and incomplete, there is a high risk of making bad decisions. In 2008, the French government established a Commission on the Measurement of Economic Performance and Social Progress to address the disconnection between GDP and economic measures and well-being. 'Moreover, it has long been clear that GDP is an inadequate metric to gauge well-being over time particularly in its economic, environmental, and social dimensions, some aspects of which are often referred to as sustainability.'[13]

GDP remains a widely quoted indicator in part because of the accounting system that underpins its design and calculation. GDP is not a result of surveying a range of businesses and households about economic activity, but an indicator that sits atop a vast accounting system that integrates data from a multitude of data sources, including financial accounts. What is called the 'income approach' to estimating GDP is based on wages and salaries + business gross operating surplus + taxes – subsidies, and 'gross operating surplus' comes from those accounts. This process sits alongside a system for national accounting with internationally agreed concepts, definitions, classifications and accounting rules. Although the information provided by company accounts is a critical input into measures of GDP, calls to change GDP have not been matched by calls to change how we account for profit.

Investment analysts' blind spot

As GDP has grown, so has the complexity of the investment market. Some investors still invest directly into businesses, but many invest into funds that pool money from many investors into a diversified portfolio. Some – for example, pension funds – own and manage such a large and diversified amount that they are described as universal owners.

For a long time now, modern portfolio theory has been the basis for investment decisions and says diversify the portfolio to reduce risk. But once you are a universal owner you can no longer diversify away systemic and systematic risk. Jon Lukomnik and Jim Hawley have argued that systemic and systematic factors – as opposed to idiosyncratic risk and return of each individual investment – influence between 75% and 94% of expected financial returns.[14] Systemic risk results from the accumulation of negative externalities. Investors have missed the role of financial accounting in calculating profits which exclude a business's contribution to externalities. If businesses are using products that depend on the use of pesticides, and those pesticides result in the reduction of pollinators, crop yields, malnutrition or even famine, then investors need to know the detail of the externalities that contribute to system-wide risks. Paying a cost for that contribution, even if small, would allow for the accumulation of externalities to be known, and for investors to make different decisions long before we reach harmful tipping points and system-wide risk. There will still be external risks, like earthquakes or meteors, but systemic risk would be a lot less.

Modern portfolio theory is also based on assumptions about rational investors, where ending up with more money than you started with is rational, irrespective of other consequences. An accounting system based on an interest that is more than just financial returns would surely be a more rational starting point. There is not much point gaining financial returns if the world around you is dying. Unless, like Ebenezer Scrooge, you prefer to spend your time counting your money.

Playing to our worst characteristics

Greed is one of the seven deadly sins, and a part of our human condition, not helped by embedded views on what is rational. It seems that however much money you have you always want more, irrespective of the damage this might do to the planet, to other people or even to yourself. And yet there is research that above a certain threshold of wealth, the effect of further increases in income to well-being start to tail off and may even become negative.[15] And this does feel intuitive. Does your well-being go up the same amount when you buy your fifth yacht as it did with the first?

But, unfortunately, accounting plays to our worst characteristics. There is no point at which the income you receive from an enterprise's profits becomes too much. It wasn't until Elon Musk's 2024 pay package rose to over US$100 billion, approved by shareholders, that a judge stepped in.[16] In a central heating system, the thermostat stops the temperature rising above a limit before the system breaks down. There is a feedback loop. There is no feedback loop in accounting. Many people see rising inequality as part of our problems and even the cause of societal breakdown,[17] but there is no point where the accounting recognizes externalities associated with increasing inequality as costs. If they were costs, this would create a feedback loop against ever increasing pay packages for a few CEOs and 'senior' managers. As Jared Diamond said, 'Perhaps our greatest distinction as a species is our capacity, unique among animals, to make counter-evolutionary choices.'[18]

David C. Rose[19] argued that competition between groups leads to larger groups. The larger groups make more deliberate decisions with 'less sympathy with harm that might come to others from our opportunistic behaviour', as the effects are distributed over a larger number of people. One element of an accounting system is an inevitable requirement to generalize the principal users of the resulting accounts so that they provide useful information. This then comes with a risk that it unintentionally legitimizes actions that have negative consequences for people that these generalized users, as a large group, do not need to account for.

Very dull

For most of us accounting is incredibly dull. It is the butt of many jokes for being so dull. Monty Python has a lot to answer for. 'It's dull, dull, dull. My God it's dull. It's so desperately dull and tedious and stuffy and boring and desperately dull.'[20]

Even the 41st[21] best stand-up comedian, Stewart Lee, has joined in.

> This doesn't normally get laughs, but I'm happy to take whatever comes from the Southend Accountants' Theatre Trip up there at the back! 'This is the bit I told you about. It's hilarious! Because presumably, he's self-employed, schedule D, but he doesn't seem to have realized that he could put the initial DVD purchase through as a tax-deductible business…' I do, right? Why is this going better than proper jokes? Just… Right, I do know that! But I put the… I put it through at the end of each quarter, not with the balance of each… It doesn't make any difference, as long as you… Who are you?! Who's come to this?![22]

If most of us think about accounting at all we see it as a simple approach to counting money. But as any accountant will tell you, it quickly stops being simple and gets very complicated. A quick glance at the financial accounts of any large corporate will give you a clue as to the complexity, and the amount of work going on behind the scenes all year round, to produce those accounts. BP's annual report in 2023 stretched to 389 pages, and the financial statements took up 138 pages of numbers. Literally, a page turner.

And it's so dull, we just accept it. We take for granted behaviours we wouldn't do in our daily lives. It becomes acceptable to buy things from suppliers who do not provide their staff with the same terms and conditions as you do in your business, or that you expect when you accept a job – because that's how business works, that's how we account for the cost of our supplies. Its dullness lull's us into actions that should be unacceptable.

Language gives a sense of security

Like any profession, accounting has its own language and complexities. Which is not a bad thing until it becomes a barrier to accountability. If you go down further into the plumbing, accounting all sounds so reasonable.[23] Any guesses what is a reasonable economic decision as compared to an unreasonable one? The 'reasonable investor' emerged from United States case law and has been used elsewhere. It helps decide what information would influence the decisions of a reasonable investor. Potentially a useful filter to stop anything and everything becoming useful or material to a decision. This framing does allow non-financial information to be material but only to the extent that it influences our decisions, made with an interest in financial returns. There is now a growing debate whether a reasonable (as well as a rational) investor would be interested in more than financial returns.[24] After all, how can it be reasonable to make decisions that generate financial returns but impose costs on other people that the investor would not accept themselves. Because it also sounds so, well, reasonable.

The very words used throughout accounting have their own poetry. Accounts must be 'true and fair', and the information must be 'faithfully represented'. It is like a romance novel: trust in me, be true to me and I will be faithful to you. Even the word 'credit', in accountant's debits and credits, relates back to the idea of personal credibility and faith, to the ability to trust someone. The use and meaning of words change over time, influenced by those who have power. Accounts can't be true if true means 100% accurate, but accounting only requires a level of accuracy that is acceptable to users; they need to be true enough. David Tweedie, an accountant, professor and the chair of the International Accounting Standards Board (IASB) between 2001 and 2011 (so he should know) is often credited with saying, 'The only thing you can rely on in a set of accounts is the date on the front.' And what about fair? True and fair has come to mean financial statements that are free from material misstatements and faithfully represent the financial performance and position of the business.

Trust is critical in all our relationships, and the operation of international markets depends on those relationships. Globally the news is not good. In 2025, the World Economic Forum's Global Risk Report identified misinformation and disinformation as the most severe short-term risk.[25] The Edelman Trust Barometer's report[26] found that '[t]he majority hold grievances against government, business, and the rich'. Sixty-one per cent globally have a moderate or high sense of grievance, defined as a belief that government and business make their lives harder and serve narrow interests – 'wealthy people benefit unfairly from the system'.

Would those surveyed trust a company's accounts? They weren't asked and unless they saw themselves as potential investors, they may not care. They may think it is too easy to 'cook the books'. What drives our sense of trust if not fairness, being fair to anyone whose lives are affected by the operations of a business. The United Nations built their Guiding Principles on Business and Human Rights[27] on the pillars of Protect, Respect and Remedy. 'Business enterprises should respect human rights. This means that they should avoid infringing on the human rights of others and should address adverse human rights impacts with which they are involved.' This includes remediation – or compensation – which would mean a business following these principles would take responsibility and recognize an obligation for those costs. It is a pity we didn't build our accounting system on the same principles; it would be a lot fairer.

Asking the wrong people

We've also been asking the wrong people. Investors, accountants and auditors have contributed to an accounting system based on the needs of those who uses accounts, rather than being based on the needs of those affected by decisions made by users of accounts.

Sustainable development means meeting the needs of current generations without compromising the needs of future generations, yet one of the ways of driving growth, and profitable companies, has been to borrow, on the basis that future generations, living in economies that have now grown, can repay – and are happy to do so. It was 2015 before the UK paid off the loan incurred to pay compensation to slavers after the 1833 Slavery Abolition Act. Would those of us whose taxes have paid off the loan have supported that decision, rather than requiring the slavers to compensate the people they had enslaved? Perhaps the public interest would be growth linked to sustainable development, and not supporting businesses that increase externalities, which would lead to more efficient resource allocation and more inclusive growth.

Even if we lived with this limitation on users, the idea that investors are interested in financial returns and only financial returns is partly because of the confusion between investment managers and investment (or asset) owners. Investment owners are the principals; investment managers look after other people's money and are their agents. Pension funds are asset owners, although even they hold the money in trust for the underlying current and future recipients of those pensions. When an investor hands over their money to investment managers, the managers ask the investor about their risk appetite and how they want to balance capital growth and earnings. But they don't ask the investor about their interest in any other types of return, or their risk appetite for risks to other people. Of course not.[28]

The purpose of accounting is presumably to provide useful information the principals and specifically those who cannot require reporting entities to provide information directly to them. How would agents know how their principals would respond to a consultation without asking them first? There is a danger that both those consulting and those consulted have forgotten that the responses are not useful unless they represent the views of the principals, are representative of all the primary users and have a transparent approach to dealing with disagreements in responses. After all, surely it is the principals who bear the economic risks and rewards – and whose expectations should be reflected. Agents could have different incentives and conflicts of interest which would lead to inefficient resource allocation. It really is of little interest to us, the principals, what the agents want.

Not an electoral issue

Fundamentally, it isn't up to accountants to decide the expectations behind how profit is calculated, despite what they may think. It is up to politicians. All countries have legislation on how companies are set up and run. And this is likely to include something about directors having to produce company accounts and set out the basis for how those accounts must be prepared. In the UK Companies Act 2006, s396 allows for the Secretary of State to require other information to be added. Making use of this provision or considering options for the basis of accounting is not top of the list of policy issues facing government and isn't a topic that comes up on the doorstep or in a Member of Parliament's mailbox. More's the pity.

Governance is complicated

Even if the accounting system hides issues with accounting in plain sight, it still ends up hiding them. One excellent way of not noticing externalities is to outsource costs to countries with lower or no legislation and buy inputs to products and services from businesses in those countries – sometimes businesses that are owned or at least controlled by the end producer. It is a sad but human reality that we buy products and services that depend on things that most of us wouldn't do personally. The coverage, accessibility and enforceability of all legislation to stop this is far from perfect, despite growing recognition of the problem in some parts of the world, for example, the European Forced Labour Regulation in 2024.[29]

If you do get close to it and start wondering whether there may be something fundamental to worry about, the complex governance structures will stop you dead in your tracks. The IASB develop and support the most internationally used accounting standards for the private sector as part of the International Financial Reporting Standards Foundation (IFRS). There is also the Financial Accounting Standards Board (FASB), as part of the Financial Accounting Foundation (FAF), whose standards are mainly used in the United States.[30] We'll focus on the IFRS Foundation, which is a private, not-for-profit, foundation set up on 1 April 2001. I kid you not. The IFRS Foundation's mission is to 'develop standards that bring transparency, accountability and efficiency to financial markets around the world'.[31] These standards do not have legal status without government endorsement or adoption, sometimes with amendments.

The IFRS oversees the work of:

- the IASB which prepares international financial reporting standards (IFRS);
- the International Financial Reporting Interpretations Committee (IFRIC),[32] which provides interpretations of those standards; and
- the work of the International Sustainability Standards Board (ISSB), which prepares standards for sustainability-related financial disclosures (and so not quite what it says on the tin which, strictly, should be ISRFDB).[33]

In turn, the IFRS Monitoring Board, drawn from the International Organization of Securities Commissions (IOSCO),[34] oversees the

IFRS Foundation. The IOSCO is the coordinating body for relevant national bodies responsible for capital markets and so has an interest in the information provided to investors. It is a not-for-profit entity initially founded under a private act sanctioned by the Québec National Assembly but moved to Madrid where it is recognized as a non-profit association under Spanish law.[35] Antonio Marcacci summarizes the IOSCO as 'multifaceted and rests upon the combination of external statutes, an autonomous General Secretariat without a founding treaty of public international law, and an intra-organization document prescribing internal rules of procedure'.[36] The relationship is set out in a Memorandum of Understanding and the Board's main responsibility is to make sure the IFRS Foundation Trustees are adhering to the IFRS Foundation Constitution.[37] Over 240 member organizations make up the IOSCO, predominantly securities regulators, and managed by a board elected from members.[38]

The public sector has its own accounting standards, developed by the International Public Sector Accounting Standards Board (IPSASB),[39] although again different jurisdictions may use their own versions of these.

On the audit side for the private sector, there is the International Foundation for Ethics and Audit (IFEA),[40] a non-profit corporation also in the United States, which oversees the International Assurance and Audit Standards Board (IAASB),[41] which sets auditing standards, and the International Ethics Standards Board for Accountants (IESBA), which supports the international code of ethics for professional accountants,[42] The Public Interest Oversight Board (PIOB)[43] oversees their work, which is the technical committee of a private foundation under Spanish law, also based in Madrid. The PIOB also appoints members to a stakeholder advisory council to provide advice and insight[44] for the IAASB and the IESBA. The PIOB's work is overseen by the Monitoring Group[45] (distinct from the IFRS Foundation Monitoring Board above) made up of the Basel Committee on Banking Supervision, the European Commission, the Financial Stability Board, the International Association of Insurance Supervisors, the International Forum of Independent Audit Regulators, the International Organization of Securities

Commissions and the World Bank. The Monitoring Group's relationship with the PIOB is managed by various documents, including the Statement on Governance and Feedback[46] and the 2020 Reform Paper.[47] Public sector auditing standards for their reporting standards are set by a personal favourite, the International Organization of Supreme Audit Institutions (INTOSAI).[48]

Then, for the accountants, there is the International Federation of Accountants (IFAC),[49] working through national accounting bodies to ensure that all these standards are properly applied by individuals and organizations with appropriate skills. At a national level the work of auditors, accountants and actuaries is overseen by financial system regulatory bodies, for example the FRC in the UK. There are several professional bodies for accountants, both global and national, including Chartered Accountants, Certified Public Accountants, Chartered Certified Accountants, Chartered Global Management Accountants, Certified Management Accountants and Chartered Public Finance Accountants.

There are other organizations involved, and apologies if I missed you, but that's enough for now.

It might look complex (even unexciting?), but it has done a good job of separating out potential conflicts of interest, making changes to support the effective operation of capital markets and the international economic system. The problem is that it can become hard to see the wood for the trees. None of these organizations are treaty organizations, where member countries have ratified a mandate, and so they do not have supranational authority. In the end, this system depends on individual governments adopting the standards and governments holding those responsible to account. Governments, in turn, are held to account by their electorates. From the perspective of a member of the electorate, accounting has become surrounded in a cloak of invisibility. What could possibly go wrong?

Public interest provides respectability

If an international organization says its work is in the public interest we can either go 'Great, that's all good then' or we can go 'Hang on, who decided what the public interest is and what happens if not all the public take the same view?' Mainly we are lulled into a false sense of security. And yet all those organizations that oversee capital markets, accounting and auditing, work in the public interest, so what the public interest is and who gets to decide it is going to be very important.

The Australian Law Reform Commission[50] concluded that '[p]ublic interest should not be defined'. Perhaps not very helpful, but it shows this is a challenging question. In the UK, the Information Commissioner's Office explanation on what the public interest covered included, 'ensuring fair commercial competition in a mixed economy'.[51]

Most of the bodies mentioned in previous paragraphs – IOSCO, IFRS, IAEF, PIOB, IPSASB, INTOSAI, FRC, IFAC and its members (e.g. the Institute of Chartered Accountants of England and Wales (ICAEW) – refer to their work being in the public interest and link that to efficient markets or similar ideas.[52] There is, though, a critical link between public interest and the avoidance and removal of externalities that we will be coming back to. Markets are efficient if there is no information asymmetry and yet can still result in externalities. However, for efficient resource allocation in markets there should be no difference between social and private returns, which means no externalities.

The ICAEW's public interest is referred to in the update to its Royal Charter in 1948[53] overseen by His Majesty's Most Honourable Privy Council, and the FRC's role as a regulator covers auditors and accountancy bodies.[54] The FRC's approach to considering the public interest[55] states that it considers the need for regulatory action to keep public confidence in accountancy and audit, corporate reporting or corporate governance. It will only act if it believes the nature, extent, sheer number or gravity of the matter is a serious public concern because it affects share prices, affects a significant number of people, has (or may have) caused financial loss or harm, or is fraudulent or unethical. We might hope that regulatory action should be coming soon, given the gravity of the issues around the accounting system, the scale of the people affected, and the financial and other losses experienced.

The International Federation of Accountants (IFAC) has an excellent policy position on 'A definition of the public interest'.[56] This defines the public interest as: 'The net benefits derived for, and procedural rigor employed on behalf of, all society in relation to any action, decision or policy.'

This is fantastic – the net benefits in relation to any action. And net means some benefits and some disbenefits – with an implicit assumption that the public interest is going to be some level of net positive. This starting point raises some critical issues. It implies that if one group receives benefits and another does not, someone has weighed these up and decided that the net is positive, or not. Of course, even then this may not be in the public interest. That interest could be that there should be a threshold, a maximum level of any negative, or the gainers should compensate the losers – especially if the public was interested in equity and fairness.

The IFAC defines both public and interest in more detail. In a section on 'Who is the public', there is reference to people whose resources *and* well-being depend on the performance of public and private institutions (emphasis added). Proof for the accountant that well-being covers more than just expected financial returns, even if not yet recognizing that well-being depends on nature and the environment, which do not 'belong' to people.

The IAASB's objective[57] is to 'serve the public interest by setting high-quality auditing, assurance, and other related standards and by facilitating the convergence of international and national auditing and assurance standards, thereby enhancing the quality and consistency of practice throughout the world and strengthening public confidence in the global auditing and assurance profession'.

The IESBA's mission is to 'serve the public interest by setting high-quality, international ethics (including independence) standards as a cornerstone to ethical behaviour in business and organizations and to public trust in financial and non-financial information that is fundamental to the proper functioning and sustainability of organizations, financial markets and economies worldwide'.

The PIOB is, 'the global independent oversight body that seeks to improve the quality and public interest focus of both international audit and assurance standards and ethics standards The PIOB's Public Interest Framework[58] states:

> All parties who have interest in international audit-related standards recognise that the public interest is best served when the standards are developed by independent, transparent and publicly accountable boards that set standards with the relevant expertise focusing on the public interest and are subject to direct oversight by an independent oversight body, which is equally focused on the public interest, ensuring that the standards appropriately address all stakeholder needs and that no undue influence is exercised by any stakeholder.

Not sure who decides what 'relevant expertise' is or who 'all the parties' are. It does look a bit like financial stakeholders are the ones with undue influence.

The IFRS Foundation and the IASB's public interest is addressed in 'Working in the Public Interest – The IFRS Foundation and the IASB.'[59] and includes bringing, 'transparency by enhancing the international comparability and quality of financial information, enabling investors and other market participants to make informed economic decisions'; strengthening accountability by, 'reducing the information gap between the providers of capital and the people to whom they have entrusted their money' and contributing to economic efficiency 'by helping investors to identify opportunities and risks across the world'. Later this is summarized as: 'Our mission statement sums up our contribution to the public interest as fostering trust, growth and long-term financial stability in the global economy.'

The IOSCO's by-laws[60] include a reference to efficient but also fair markets, stating that it works, '[t]o ensure market structures do not unduly favour some users over others and that investors are given fair and transparent access to market facilities or price information on a real-time basis'. And, '[t]o promote and allow for the effective management of risk and ensure that capital requirements are sufficient to address appropriate risk taking and allow for the absorption of some losses'. Their role is determined by the members, so perhaps the basis for the IOSCO's public interest sits with the members. The UK's Financial Conduct Authority (FCA) is one of those members. The FCA is a company limited by guarantee (a form of private company, a not for profit) and '[t]he FCA's Mission is to serve the public interest through the objectives given to it by Parliament'.[61] The FCA's public interest comes from the Financial Services and Markets Act 2000, which sets out those objectives and is held to account by HM Treasury. All very good until we remember that there are more than 130 members of IOSCO, each presumably accountable for a public interest.

This is all very complex. It might help promote transparency to have more clarity on their public interest statements, how each organization has determined that interest and how anyone might hold them to account. It was hard enough to see the wood for the trees with all the governance before adding in the public interest and considering the chain of accountability. It might even help if all this was brought together under an international treaty with clear mandates and accountability.

Conclusion to Part 1

For a wide range of reasons, we have not acknowledged that the accounting system allows directors to prepare, and auditors to accept, accounts that exclude costs caused by a business. The focus on legally enforceable obligations – for example, contracts or taxes – as a source of costs means that other costs are not included – even though they still exist. These costs are what become externalities and have reached a scale across climate, nature, inequality and social justice that they are undermining society.

Directors and auditors do not see the absence of the costs that are imposed on others as a question of morals, it is just a consequence of applying accounting standards. A practice that has normalized behaviours that we would never, or at least most of us would never, follow in our personal relationships.

This is all classic hegemony, the process by which control is maintained with consent of those controlled. We have consented to an approach to calculating profit for some, at the same time as imposing costs on the rest of us. This might be in the short-term interest of an entrepreneur or an investor as they make more money, though many of these costs will come back to bite them as much as they bite everyone else. It might be in the interest of the very rich, who have enough wealth and power to offset any negative consequences for themselves, but it is not in our wider public interest. As Foucault said, 'Each society has its regime of truth, its "general politics" of truth: that is, the types of discourse which it accepts and makes function as true…',[1] which includes accounting standards and the legislative context in which they operate. Once calculated, profit becomes a form of knowledge that becomes the accepted truth.

Most of the current solutions to our economic and social challenges leave the calculation of profit untouched, adding further accretions to our wider economic system and burying the problem a little bit deeper and a little bit harder to see.

And so we missed it.

Though not everyone has. In 2013, Peter Bakker, the CEO of the World Business Council for Sustainable Development (WBCSD), said that accountants would save the world and that we needed to change accounting rules.[2] In 2021, the WBCSD released its Vision 2050,[3] arguing for internalizing social and environmental costs and benefits. And in 2021, the ICAEW argued that 'it was time for accountants to save the world'.[4] Meanwhile Philippe Joubert, the former President of Alstom Power and Deputy CEO of Alstom Group and founder of Earth on Board, said, 'So I defend the thesis that the profit that we are declaring is fake, summarizing when I don't have time I say, we are all counterfeiters.'[5]

Part 2

How did we come to this?

If we are going to come up with solutions, we need to understand how we came to this state of affairs and the history that led to our current accounting system.[1] We need to understand how this developed within a wider system by which society holds us all to account for our actions, creating inescapable obligations. This wider system has never been perfect but now, in the face of rising inequality, it is at breaking point.

Accounting has been around for a very long time but the current approach has its roots in the eleventh century, developed during 'the age of exploration' in the seventeenth and the shift to a capitalist economy in the eighteenth and became formalized through the nineteenth to twentieth centuries. These periods are also convenient periods to focus on the types of costs that are being met by people and the planet, and that have become known as externalities; costs experienced by women, enslaved people and colonialization, resulting from mining and the exploitation of nature. These are costs of climate change, biodiversity loss, unpaid labour and exploitative working practices. The S&P Global report referenced earlier included some of these in its estimate of US$3.7 trillion.

It was rich men, and especially rich white men in Europe, owning property and making investments, that were able to develop the philosophies, legal systems and techniques so they could choose what costs to include and ignore many of the consequences of their actions. They and their families became wealthy in the process and embedded a system that would continue to generate and justify wealth inequality, with the costs being borne by the least well off. This means that the problem of how some costs are in financial accounts and others are not, lies in the history of Europe and the United States. The solution is far more international, but it takes less space to set out possible solutions than to understand the cause. Other options were possible. Islamic accounting had a different basis, with a focus on the community rather than an individual investor.[2] Equally, in Balinese Hindu accounting, the tenets of Tat Twam Asi prioritize togetherness and a belief that happiness through trade is not always measured by monetary gain. However, the international accounting system developed alongside an economic system that prioritizes individual financial returns.

Each chapter in this part considers the general changes to how society considered accountability, an example of a significant externality, plus related developments in financial accounting. It is a story of how the accountability system has failed as society changed, costs increased and accounting developed. Society has not held those organizations that are creating these costs to account.

The starting point is the eleventh century. It would always be possible to start an analysis of how societies have held people to account earlier, but the eleventh century is a time picked for when changes in Europe set the tone for today's global approach to financial accounting.[3]

Chapter 3

Eleventh to sixteenth century

Changes in accountability

In the eleventh century, as today, people (as individuals, not yet as businesses) were held to account for their actions through a mix of social, religious and legal structures. The important shift was the emergence of formal ways in which kings and queens could be held to account as well. The primary source of accountability was religion, and it is hard to imagine living in a world with so much uncertainty where belief in God and the Devil was ubiquitous and where religion permeated every moment of your day. For everyone, God was the final arbiter, holding us all to account for our actions and our faith, though only after our death, on Judgement Day, 'For he has set a day when he will judge the world with justice by the man he has appointed' (Acts 17.13).

There was also purgatory to worry about. Purgatory was a big thing – that intermediate state of unknown duration for purifying a soul that might take thousands of years. Fortunately, there was much you could do to reduce the time spent there. You could be granted an 'indulgence' in return for some compensatory action like prayer or a pilgrimage for your sins. There was no list of how much time you could get taken off for different types of good behaviour until it became possible to pay for an indulgence, and a market rate for a year in purgatory emerged. This is a very early approach to paying compensation for sins, for harm done, with the payment going to God, via the church.

Abelard and Heloise were twelfth century philosophers and lovers. They argued that intention determined the moral value of human action. Heloise wrote, 'For it is not the deed itself but the intention of the doer that makes the sin. Equity weighs not what is done, but the spirit in which it is done.'[1] Ironic, since the proverb ascribed to Saint Bernard of Clairvaux (also twelfth century) says 'Hell is full of good intentions or wishes'.[2] Under Islam it was a bit clearer, with weighing being done on the scales of justice on Judgement Day. Not just the number of good and bad deeds but also their weight. No 'materiality' thresholds here. A deed was relevant and therefore included, 'So whoever does an atom's weight of good will see it, and whoever does an atom's weight of evil will see it.'[3] Good deeds must outweigh bad deeds, and the weighing would be just and fair.

This all made the questions of how to decide good or bad actions a critical concern, for both people and for how religious faiths provided people's spiritual guidance. One of the good actions has always been charity, helping others in more need than yourself, selflessly. Not necessarily recognizing that the position of those in need may arise, in part, from your actions, but at least recognizing that, but for the grace of God, you might be in that same boat.

People were providing products and services, and these need to be accounted for. Inevitably, accounting was focusing on intended consequences, what had been sold to someone and what had been bought from someone else – and whether the income was higher than the costs. This ranged from relatively simple to very complex accounting requirements, from making clothes to building cathedrals, to managing wars. For any of these, having a contract helped to manage the risks and meant that, in the event of the contract not being met, one of the parties could resort to the law. In England, this was the common law, law by judges rather than written codes.

Intent was important, and today a legally binding contract requires those involved to intend to create legal relations. But focusing on intent comes with a big risk. The more we focus on intent the less we focus on unintended consequences. We may forget that whether or not there was intent is not very important to those experiencing the consequences.

Up until William the Conqueror succeeded in his claim to become King of England, a mix of the King's Court, local courts, such as the manor courts, and ecclesiastical courts ran the country's justice system. As everything changed, justice became centralized. The Court of Common Pleas handled disputes between subjects under a standardized system of law. This was common law, common to all subjects, and as it became more complex it could result in decisions that a plaintiff considered unjust. In the absence of other options, all a plaintiff could do was petition the King. The King's Council handled all this, but, even with the inevitable restrictions on who could petition, the Council had too much else to do and delegated it all to the Lord Chancellor. Not unreasonably perhaps, since the Chancellor was the Keeper of the King's Conscience.[4] The first Lord Chancellor was Thomas à Beckett in 1155, appointed by Henry II. Whether with the King's intent or not, Thomas was assassinated. Henry had to pay compensation and had his work cut out to recover his reputation. As well as walking barefoot through Canterbury as a penance, he financed and supported several abbeys as well as St Mary's Church in Dover and Trinity Chapel within Canterbury Cathedral. Even kings could be held to account for their actions, intended or otherwise.

The Chancellor's work came under the Chancery, which became a court dealing with injustices arising from application of the common law. Over time, this became equity law. Accounting focused on transactions in contracts that came under common law. The separation between common and equity law is one of the reasons that accounting has developed to focus on some costs, recorded at a particular level of certainty (common law) and exclude other costs that might accept or require a lower level of certainty (equity law). Intent and intended costs in contracts are more certain. Lack of intent and unintended costs are harder to claim, bring to law and gain redress.

Thomas Aquinas was a Dominican Friar writing in Aquino in Italy in the thirteenth century who was far ahead of his time. If anyone was thinking about accounting and accountability, it was Thomas. Among many ideas, he developed the idea of a just price,[5] a price that should reflect the cost of production, a reasonable profit and the common good. His cost of production included the cost of materials and a fair living for workers, enough to support a family. These are still costs relating to transactions between parties that have an agreement. The other costs, the ones imposed on those who had not agreed and were not receiving anything in consideration, might be included in his ideas for the common good. His thinking has gone on to influence many of the ways in which markets are regulated for a common good and protect us from those (hopefully) unintended consequences, including protecting consumers' rights and ensuring competitive markets.[6]

The idea that there might be other costs that people[7] experience, that might be unintended, was recognized, but not so easy to do something about. At least society did recognize that they were costs and provide some way, at least for the lucky few, to seek compensation. Holding those responsible to account when neither those causing the consequences nor those experiencing them were aware was harder to grapple with. The costs still arise, harm was being done and society found ways to address that harm. One way was by paying tithes, giving one-tenth of your income to religious organizations. Those organizations that will be your guide to good or bad actions, and how you might recover from any bad actions, need financial support. They are also potentially an effective way of supporting people in need. Like it or not, paying tithes was going to help you get to heaven. And some of those tithes would help people in need, which would also help you get to heaven. Charlemagne (r. 768–814) had already made tithes compulsory for everyone across his realm, covering much of modern-day France, Germany, Belgium, the Netherlands and northern Italy. William I made tithes compulsory for landowners in the eleventh century. The dissolution of the monasteries between 1536 and 1541 meant that the rights to raise tithes were transferred or sold to landowners, with the requirement to support the poor being conveniently dropped.

Making payments as a religious obligation is not limited to Christianity. Zakat is one of the five pillars of Islam, and it is a religious obligation for all Muslims that meet a wealth threshold

Figure 3.1: St Thomas of Aquinas

Source: *Saint Thomas Aquinas*, painting by Carlo Crivelli, 15th century. Collection of the National Gallery, London. Image sourced from Wikimedia Commons, public domain. Available at: https://commons.wikimedia.org/wiki/File:St-thomas-aquinas.jpg

to pay 2.5%. It became mandatory after the Prophet Muhammad migrated to Medina in 622 CE. In Judaism there is Ma'aser, where 10% of income is given for religious and social purposes. Sikhism has Dasvandh and an expected voluntary 10%. Hinduism and Buddhism have the idea of Dana, selfless giving as a spiritual duty, with no fixed amount. And while Islam's 2.5% may be less than a more common 10%, it is based on wealth not income.

Just as religious authorities needed money so did royalty, which has always spent time finding ways to increase tax receipts, starting with making sure they know what everyone owns. The Domesday Book did just that and was well-named as a reference back to Judgement Day. One of the reasons Europe's royalty needed more money was the Crusades, and taxation was not going to be enough. Plunder, mortgages, personal wealth and loans were all needed. Unfortunately, the Church was totally opposed to charging interest on loans, or usury, which was a bit of problem. The decrees of the Fourth Lateran Council of 1215 meant excommunication for both unrepentant usurers, and princes, who failed to suppress usury. It also established two preaching orders – the Franciscans and the Dominicans – who forecast a bad end for presumed usurers. This led to new forms of finance, especially the use of annuities. In 1250 Pope Innocent IV conveniently ruled that 'rentes', the purchase of the rights to future income streams, was not usury.[8] All of which made for a more complex financial system. Which needs someone, an accountant perhaps, to keep track of all these transactions and people to manage the financial flows, perhaps a merchant banker. There was not much chance for any of those other non-contracted costs to get a look in.

Borrowing money was not only a problem for royalty. Increasing credit had consequences for anyone who couldn't pay. Often for small amounts, debtors might end up in prison until someone had paid off their debt. In England, it wouldn't be until the 1869 Debtors Act that there was a legal limit on how long you might spend there. Most of the religious equivalents of tithes allowed for the relief of debts. For example, under ancient Jewish Law, all debts were cancelled every 50 years.[9] And debt relief is specifically recognized in the Qur'an: 'Alms are for the poor and the needy, and those employed to administer [funds]; for those whose hearts have been reconciled to truth; for those in bondage and in debt…'[10]

Between 1347 and 1351 Europe was wracked by the Black Death with between 30% and 50% of the population dying, all wrapped around the additional challenges, for some, of the Hundred Years' War. One of the consequences of the plague was that the economic position of peasants improved, as wages increased rapidly, bringing the end to serfdom and the rise of free farmers. Kings and Queens increasingly had to rely on mercenaries or paid soldiers to fight their wars. In the 1500s, the response to wage increases was the enclosure of land and an increase in the number of landless peasants. Workers were separated from the means of production, from around 90% working on the land in the early fourteenth century to around 60% by the late sixteenth century. This was also a separation of people from the landlords,[11] who had previously borne some responsibility for the people living on their estates. It was out of the frying pan into the fire. Now, if you were unemployed, you were on your own. Or those costs had been externalized, depending how you look at it.

So, there were ways to ensure (some) people were held to account for the consequences of their actions, remembering that it was people and not yet businesses that were being held to account. The other costs, external to this system of accounting under common law, may seem relatively small, at least to the extent that the whole system wasn't being threatened.

A fourteenth-century externality

Externalities, costs imposed by those who can on those who cannot enforce payment, are generally experienced by poorer people, but even then rarely equitably. There was one group of people experiencing many consequences of the actions of another group who had even less ability to hold them to account. Women. Although this was neither a good time for most people to be either a man or a woman, women bore the brunt of these costs. People were now a cost of production, a cost to be minimized and, if possible, a cost to be ignored. The amount paid was limited to the direct work done. Indirect work (i.e., in the household) was created but not recognized. Direct and indirect work was divided between men and women and, as Silvia Federici puts it:

> But in the new organisation of work every woman (other than those privatised by bourgeois men) became a communal good, for once women's activities are defined as non-work, women's labour began to appear as a natural resource, available to all, no less than the air we breathe or the water we drink.[12]

People become divided based on competitive advantage, where women's competitive advantage was that they are the means of production of labour. Their separation from paid work was intensified, and social and legal expectations on marriage and childbirth meant that the costs of supporting current and future paid workers could be ignored. Where women *did* gain paid work, they could be paid less, setting in stone the pay inequality that continues to this day. Women's role was to have children, and sexual practices were only acceptable if they could lead to pregnancy.[13] Federici again: 'The sexual division of labour that emerged from it not only fixed women to reproductive work, but increased their dependence on men, enabling the state and employers to use the male wage as a means to command women's labour.'[14]

And so, the costs imposed on women started building up. Unpaid labour, domestic abuse and rape, restriction to choice and agency, servitude, death in labour, the list goes on, the total amount of externalized cost, stolen from women's lives, mounts up. Women had long been external to commerce and to the 'economy'. The increasing number of women who defied this and rose above and fought for their independence did not change the general experience. Neither does it suggest that women were passive or not involved in a struggle for their rights. But the costs imposed on women were the most significant externality of this time and were in addition to those affecting men.

One way of holding people to account is through education but women could not attend university even though Fatima al-Fihri had founded the first university in the world, the University of al-Qarawiyyin in Morocco, in 859 CE. A few did manage. Bettisia Gozzadini[15] earned a law degree from the University of Bologna in 1237, some time before Elena Piscopia earned her PhD from the University of Padua in 1678. These are all exceptional women, running very much against the grain. For other women, the best opportunity for an education was to be a nun, until nunneries were closed across Protestant Europe and the life of a nun was more regulated in other regions. The legal system meant that most women's access to education and justice was a different story.

Coverture limited women's involvement in contracts. Under common law, her legal identity, her property and her earnings all became 'covered' by her husband on marriage.[16] She could only enter contracts with her husband's permission. If she was yet to marry, a 'feme sole' as opposed to a 'feme covert', then she could own property, sue and be sued, but marriage was the expected state. Her rights and status – legal, educational, marriage, health, clothing, leadership, travel and inheritance – were all fewer than men's and all determined by men.

Figure 3.2: Bettisia Gozzadini

Source: *Bettisia Gozzadini*, lithograph by A. Nepoti, from Cenni biografici e ritratti d'insigni donne bolognesi by Carolina Bonafede, Bologna: Sassi, 1845. Image sourced from Wikimedia Commons, public domain. Available at: https://commons.wikimedia.org/wiki/File:Bettisia_Gozzadini,lithograph_from_Carolina_Bonafede,Cenni_biografici%E2%80%A6,_1845.jpg

There is now much more research on how women were able to act and transact. Research on court cases[17] shows that women had more involvement in the legal system than previously thought, though care needs to be taken as to whether they were litigants or defendants, involved with their husbands or on their behalf, or dealing with issues around inheritance. In the UK, in the case of Chancery and equity law, women's involvement was around 20%, which increased to more than 40% by the reign of James 1.[18] It was probably higher in the ecclesiastical courts, given that these considered cases relating to marriage, divorce, sexual conduct, adultery and defamation. But the judges and the lawyers were, of course, all men. Had there been equal access, especially in cases relating to liability for costs, then there would be more case law and more precedent that reflected women's experience and context. There wasn't, and so bias is hardwired into our legal system and our laws.

Although coverture meant the married women's rights were already curtailed, there was now an erosion of rights of non-married women. The assault on women reduced access to public spaces and differentiated men and women; between reason and unreason.[19]. If the violence of the period was endemic, it was worse for women. Legitimized by religion and the state, it peaked during the witch hunts and the death of perhaps 60,000 women across Europe, deaths only possible with new legislation.

A struggle arose between people with only their labour to sell and people who owned other resources – e.g. land, rights to trade or enslaved people. The contractor bore little or no responsibility for costs outside those agreed in the contract and no longer had a responsibility for systemic costs arising from periods where there was no work. And financial accounting legitimized it all, creating an inescapable norm out of the subjugation of labour and the subjugation of women for reproduction of the labour force. Or in today's language – a dependency: a resource on which a business is dependent but does not have to pay for (at all or in full).

For all these religious and cultural reasons, it might just about be understandable how men came to exclude the unique costs imposed on women from society's approach to accountability. And it is probably obvious, given the power imbalances between royalty and serfs, that the justice system wasn't really designed for the serfs, whether men or women. This is not about missing costs. It is about repressed costs – and continues to this day.

Developments in financial accounting

According to Christine de Pisan, a woman writing about accounting between 1410 and 1414 in *The Treasure of the City of Ladies*, proper account-keeping was a religious duty allowing women to ensure their husbands' accumulated wealth was used for justifiable purposes.[20] Book-keeping was just another of those jobs that was part of a woman's household duties, of whatever class, although wealthier women would be able to employ someone to help – with their husband's agreement. Religion was still the arbiter of which costs were justifiable and therefore recognized, and how they were addressed.

These decisions were the basis for the systems, laws and standards designed to protect individuals and societies from the consequences of those costs, but designed by men, and excluding accountability for those costs imposed on women. Which only set women up for the consequences that follow.

Financial accounting ended up focusing on transactions between buyers and sellers. Items with a high level of certainty, relating to goods and services that exist and where ownership and existence could generally be supported by physical and written evidence. Contracts often provided some clarity on who is doing what and when and for whom.

Alongside other social and economic changes, the Black Death had significant implications for accounting. Handling inflation was, and is, a major bug bear – any delays between when you pay for something and when you get paid can quickly become the difference between profit and loss. Hyperinflation is what makes taxis cheaper than buses as you pay for the taxi at the end of the journey. After the plague came wage inflation, the need for new types of contracts to handle wage increases, problems in supply chains, increases in unpaid debts, the high level of transfers in property and changes to the value of estates. Improvements in accounting practice followed.

The need for tighter control over financial transactions encouraged the use of the newly invented double-entry book-keeping. A common view is that Italian merchants drove its use, but it was universities that started it off, places of learning where most accountants were trained and where the use of numerals was more common.[21] They were still religious institutions and, influenced by Abelard's thinking about inquiry as a route to truth, universities shifted to using examinations to recognize expertise, including expertise in their own accounting. Most importantly, the accounts were literally heard. Audit, as a form of inquisition of the stewardship of a university's land, considered what should have happened. As accounting developed, men become the accountants and women were still the bookkeepers.[22]

This is still early days for accounting. The focus on transactions between individuals made the differentiation between accountability under common law and accountability under equity law inevitable. A line was drawn that informed decisions on which costs should be included in the accounts.

Chapter 4

Seventeenth to eighteenth century

Changes in accountability

This period is also known as the Age of Exploration, although this has got to be in the running for the most misnamed period of history, exploring places that the existing residents had already explored (and lived in). And when you get there taking everything you can lay your hands on or, if you had to pay, paying far less than a just price. This is the Age of Grand Larceny. And religion, primarily in the form of the Catholic Church, was at the heart of all this.

At the end of the fourteenth century, Pope Alexander VI had decided to carve up the world between Portugal and Spain.[1] The deal was that they would have to convert the people who lived there to Christianity and so save their souls. By the beginning of the seventeenth century, Spain was the richest country in Europe and trading was becoming very complicated. Equipping and sending a ship full of trade goods around the world was expensive, returns could be high, but so were the risks. Ways for groups of people to work together – for example, the Medieval Guilds, sharing income, costs and risks – had been around for some time, but the rise of the joint stock company was a critical development. A joint stock company was a one where ownership could be divided between people owning a share, or a stock, representing a claim on a part of the assets and earnings of a company. A structure that would help lose sight of some of the costs of running a business. The first capital market that covered the sale and purchase of stocks and bonds (a form of loan) was started in Holland to finance the activities of the Dutch East India and West India companies. Other countries were quick to follow suit, pursuing markets that were hardly arms-length transactions between equal parties, where trade and the musket went hand in hand.

Perhaps the poster child for these activities became the English East India Company. The Company's first governor was an accountant, Sir Thomas Smythe. He was there from its launch in 1600 until 1621 – except for 1606 to 1607, when he was appointed receiver for the Duchy of Cornwall, and 1609 when he also became treasurer for the Virginia Company in America.[2] His skills and perspectives would shape the future of company structure and governance along with the future of finance. Busy man. Under-recognized.

Figure 4.1: Thomas Smythe

Source: *Sir Thomas Smythe*, engraving by Simon van de Passe, 1617. Collection of the National Portrait Gallery, London. Image sourced from Wikimedia Commons, public domain. Available at: https://commons.wikimedia.org/wiki/File:Sir_Thomas_Smythe.jpg

Initially, the East India Company treated each trading voyage as a separate venture and, at the end of each voyage, the profit, or loss, was calculated and shared between investors. The first voyage in 1601 consisted of four ships, and investors nearly doubled their money. Over time the Company shifted to a continuous investment model, where investors could either roll over their capital, the money they had invested, to new but specific voyages, or withdraw it. In

1657 it became a permanent joint-stock corporation as part of Oliver Cromwell's renewal of its Charter. This was the legal structure in place when the company presided over the Bengal Famine and the death of 10 million people,[3] while charging land taxes and forcing production of cash crops. Externalities at scale.

The disconnection between an individual's and a business's responsibility and accountability was now well underway. A business is, after all, responsible for pursuing the financial interest of the owners. Directors were still legally responsible for a company's debts, unless protected by government exemptions, but it was accepted that directors and employees might act in ways completely different from how they would act as individuals following the Golden Rule. In *Charitable Corporation v Sutton 1742*, directors were characterized as having duties similar to both trustees and agents, underpinning the emergence of directors' fiduciary duties and the duty to promote the company's success – and so externalize costs. Rather different from how Paul Polman tried to run Unilever two centuries later: 'We are going to say that these are the issues in society that we don't accept. We will fight very hard to get them out of our system. And the basic driver is that I would not want to be treated like that.'[4]

English equity law was still around but the different level of certainty used was still an issue. A seventeenth-century jurist, John Selden, said, 'Equity is a roguish thing: for law we have a measure, know what to trust to; equity is according to the conscience of him that is Chancellor, and as that is larger or narrower, so is equity.' One example of a law under equity that still exists is the law of unjust enrichment.[5] A claim of unjust enrichment requires one party to a contract to have been enriched at the expense of another where this is unjust and for which there is no defence. If a company CEO earning several million a year were directly employing someone on a low salary in the business, below a living wage, that might seem like unjust enrichment. But it would not be grounds for a claim as, unfortunately, it is the company that is the employer, not the CEO.

A seventeenth-century externality

These externalities underpin the creation of products and services that continue to cause problems today. The next convenient exclusion of cost might be explicable but is even harder to understand. In the Americas and Asia, trade wasn't just a case of taking and shipping silver and gold or even buying spices. Land needed to come under control of the 'visitors'. Described as colonies by those who had invaded, they legitimized control by enforcing rules and structures, often justified by religion. Gold and silver weren't just lying around, someone had to dig it out, 'someone' often being enslaved people. Slavery has of course been around for a very long time. Rome might not have been built in a day, but it was built by slaves and, over in Greece, Aristotle even believed that some people were natural slaves. By the seventeenth century, as the land under control of European countries expanded, the morality and legality of enslaving people became more of an issue, but so did the potential for enslaving ever more people.

Using enslaved people who didn't have to be paid was obviously going to be more profitable, which wasn't going to sit well with Thomas Aquinas or with the Catholic Church in general. Even in the previous period, Popes had tried to stem the flow, starting with Pope Eugene in 1434 issuing a Papal Bull excommunicating anyone who enslaved newly converted Christians from the Canary Islands.[6] He had another go a year later, but this still only addressed the Canary Islands. The debate then became about whether people could enslave Christians, which was going to be a problem given the people doing the slaving were also supposed to be doing the converting. Eight years earlier, Pope Clement VII made this more confusing by giving Charles V the authority to use force to help convert Indigenous people.[7] In 1537, Pope Paul III issued a Papal Bull, Sublimis Deus, that condemned enslaving converted Indigenous peoples… but was ignored.

There does not appear to be an example of a Pope excommunicating anyone for enslaving people, though we might assume they spent, perhaps are still, spending time in Purgatory. For anyone who wanted to carry on without risking the future of their soul, the solution was to use the Just War doctrine.[8] This doctrine basically allowed war to be declared if there was a wrong that the responsible party refused to address. Just as a state could act against citizens, with force, if they broke the law, so a state could act against other states that broke the law. Given it was the right of Portugal and Spain to be trading and a requirement that they converted Indigenous people, it followed, as night follows day, that anyone resisting conversion or trading was breaking the law and could be legally enslaved.

Not that any of this mattered in England, where it was the Anglican Church that decided such things. And was as inconsistent, even defending the practice by falling back on the Bible for support.[9] 'As for your male and female slaves whom you may have – you may acquire male and female slaves from the pagan nations that are around you.'[10] Just as well, as by the mid-sixteenth century, the population of Indigenous people in the 'New World' had collapsed from disease and violence, and demand was outrunning supply. One thing was clear. While you might have to pay to buy your slaves, you wouldn't have to pay them for their loss of liberty, for their work, for being torn from home and family or for their reduced life expectancy.

Enslaving people was big business. Research by Klass Ronnback[11] suggests that by the end of the eighteenth century it had grown from 3% to 11% of the UK economy. It was even more important for the economy of the United States. By the start of the Civil War,[12] as much as 60% of its exports came from cotton grown and harvested by enslaved people. In 1790, the first United States Census recorded that for every 100 free white people there were 53 enslaved people.[13] As the historian Edward Baptist points out, until the beginning of the Civil War, 'The Slave economy of the US South is deeply tied financially to the North, to Britain, to the point that we can say that people who were buying financial products in these other places were in effect owning slaves, and were extracting money from the labour of enslaved people.'[14]

Or as Akala puts it in *Natives: Race and Class in the Ruins of Empire*:[15]

> It wasn't free trade or open markets but military rule, forced servitude, national monopolies and absolutely no semblance of democracy that helped modern Europe and America to develop. Racism gave slave owners the justification for

> an unprecedented experiment in the denial of liberty and forced servitude and this racism, far from being marginal or just a side effect, has been absolutely central to developing Euro-American prosperity.

It is not surprising that financial accounting developed so that the cost experienced by enslaved people could be ignored. With free market ideology writ large in the selective perspective of Adam's Smith invisible hand, and a collective need to justify the level of exploitation that underpinned those markets, it is hard to see how it would have been different. If these costs had been included, many businesses would not have started. They made profits but nothing like enough to have covered all these excluded costs. In an account of the history of the Liverpool slave trade,[16] Gomer Williams includes an analysis of the profit in pounds shillings and pence (see Table 4.1).

It feels uncomfortable to be writing this down, let alone imagining a clerk somewhere doing the same, inured to the practice, never wondering how these figures could be just, true or fair. Forgetting that the real cost was far more than the 9 pounds 8 shillings and 5 pence in Table 4.1 below and the business should have been recording a loss. This is a problem with reparations. The profits were never enough to pay back the full costs, even if the money had been put aside. It is hard to estimate the amount that would be required but in *From Here to*

Table 4.1: An analysis of profit from buying and selling a person

Net proceeds of one slave to be		£40 9 6 ¾
Prime cost of one slave on the coast	27 5 10	27 5 10
Freight of one slave	3 5 3¾	
The maintenance of one slave	0 10 0	
		31 1 1¾
Profit on the sale of one slave		£9 8 5

Equality: Reparations for Black Americans in the Twenty-First Century, authors Darity and Mullen consider several estimates, some going as high as US$14 trillion[17] for a specific period in American history.

One thing is sure: now, as then, we are all still buying things made or supplied by people who are not being paid the rate that most of us would pay or want to be paid. That difference is still a cost, imposed on people not getting anywhere near fair wages, but also for all of us, as our morals are eroded, and the Golden Rule is not so much of a rule at all.

As if this wasn't all bad enough, then there are the products being grown in this period by enslaved people. The big two were sugar and cotton. Sugar went on to be the primary cause of obesity, a product of no nutritional value. Some 1 in 8 people in the world were obese in 2022,[18] and yes, sugar intake contributes to body weight.[19] Cotton has become one of the biggest users of water requiring 2,700 litres for a t-shirt and using 16% of annual global use of pesticides with resulting damage to the ecosystem.[20]

It was not only taking people from their land. It was also taking land from the people who stayed. So much land was taken. Some of it returned when countries gained independence, some of it never really returned in full.[21] Some of it now paid for – in part. The Māori are an example of successful negotiation with their new governments. In a series of Treaty of Waitangi settlements, they have managed to sign agreements for NZ$2.6 billion.[22] Not bad. Until you realize that in 2020 the COVID 19 Wage Subsidy scheme paid out over NZ$14 billion,[23] of which around NZ$2 billion was in the first two weeks. Not so good. And all that risks forgetting that the bulk of the 'value' generated by using that land didn't stay in New Zealand. It went to the UK, under terms of trade that provided competitive advantage and supported wealth concentration while ignoring costs. Perhaps the repayment should have come from somewhere else?

Until the eighteenth century the middle class was a very small proportion of the total population. Then industrialization, colonialism and enslaving other people massively increased demand for new specialized skills operating between the producer and the consumer – mostly a middleman, often administrative, sometimes accountants.

This marked the end of feudalism and the rise of the bourgeoisie. The rise of people whose wealth was not tied to land, but to trade and to money. Money that now needed to do something, which brings us to the increase in investing and to secondary markets for those investments, to stock exchanges.

Developments in financial accounting

The development of the joint stock company and permanent investment meant big changes for accounting. This was the time of the major shift from book-keeping to accounting and audit. Keeping capital in the business meant that income and costs would have to be allocated between different time periods. Just because you had been paid cash didn't mean it paid for this year's trading activities; it might be a payment in advance for next year. Just because you had cash in the bank didn't mean it could be distributed to investors; it might be needed to pay next year's obligations. You might owe money to your suppliers, to people who have lent you money, or to people who have invested, and might lose the lot, but are 'owed' any profits. This is where the idea of the primary users of financial accounts comes from – these three groups of 'creditors' – investors, lenders and other creditors (e.g. suppliers) – are the people or businesses who are listed in the credit side of your double-entry accounts.

You will also need to have money reserved for next year's trading, to provide a cushion for unforeseen events. Then there are all sorts of conflicts to be managed, investors who are suppliers, who overcharge, investors who are managers, who overpay themselves. All of which became more common as trade grew. This reserve of capital had grown by making profit, by generating income and 'minimizing' costs. One way of reducing costs, especially as workers started to organize how to improve their wages, was to replace them with 'capital' – that is, with machinery where the cost had been 'capitalized'. Yes, labour is embodied in the machinery but, as importantly, any costs relating to externalities are also disembodied from the machinery. The externalities are hidden deeper within the machine. Accounting creates incentives to replace labour with 'machines', whether digital or otherwise, and concentrates wealth in the hands of a few. The dual use of the word 'capital' is also potentially confusing. One use represents the money invested in a company and is its 'capital'; the other represents expenditure that will generate economic benefits for more than one accounting period and so is 'capitalized'.

The expansion in trade and slow relaxation of usury laws increased the demand for credit. Trade also requires investment with more risk, which led to new company structures. The system for financing these activities also became more complex. And this sets me up for my favourite accountant: Matthaus Schwarz. Matthaus was Jacob Fugger's accountant and Jacob was the Hapsburg Dynasty's banker and one of the richest men of all time. Hard to see how Matthaus managed to keep on top of everything without any accounting software, let alone without AI. Matthaus had enough time to publish the first book on fashion,[24] a book of the clothes he wore between 1520 and 1560. Proof, should you need it, that accountants are not boring. One thing Matthaus *didn't* do was hold Jacob to account for his belief that 'I am rich by god's grace without injury to any man'.[25]

Figure 4.2: Matthaus Schwarz

Source: *Matthäus Schwarz at age 19*, anonymous 16th-century watercolor from the "Klaidungsbüchlein" (Book of Clothes). Image sourced from Wikimedia Commons, public domain. Available at: https://commons.wikimedia.org/wiki/File:Matthaus_19_years.jpg

A couple of the East India Company's accounts have survived. Article 306 of the East India Company's bylaws, published in 1621, states that, 'They [Accountants General] shall yearely deliver up unto the Court [of Committees] at the Fine of June, a perfect Ballance of all Accompts in their charge.' To ensure the reliability of the annual report, the Auditors General of the Company were instructed to 'have care of the general accompts, to see that all the other accompts and parcels be fairely and truly entered into them by the Bookekeepers'.[26]

Two things stand out. For fans of a perfect Manhattan, the way the word 'perfect' is used to describe a balance sheet will now never leave you. More importantly, this is probably the first recorded reference to an idea that will become fundamental in company reporting all over the world. The information should be 'fairely and truly' entered, the precursor of the requirement that the accounts should give a true and fair view. It is easy to see why ensuring that information was 'fairely and truly' entered would be a problem. Just think of some of the issues. The line of communication was extremely long and local book-keeping records were often incomplete. Timings of voyages – especially if, at the date of the accounts, some were in progress and others still had some of the assets in a warehouse – added complexity, plus there may be an increasing number of shareholders. Keeping true and fair accounts may have seemed insurmountable but accounting steps up.

Here is John Mair writing an accounting manual in 1741,[27]

> Thus, if he be a Merchant who deals in proper Trade, he ought to know, by inspecting his Books, to whom he owes, and who owes him; what Goods he has purchased; what he has disposed of, with the Gain or Loss upon; the Sale, and what he has yet on hand; what Goods or Money he in the Hands of Factors; what ready Money he has by him; what his Stock was at first; what Alterations and Changes it has suffered since, and what it now amounts to.

The books are enough to know what is owed, but this still depends on whether they are a complete record.

Accounting moves further away from a more holistic and individual approach to being accountable for the consequences of transactions. The increase in lending, allowing money to be spent now and repaid from expected future returns is a fundamental shift. Achieving the financial return to pay loans is critical, almost irrespective of other consequences. Separating the company from the individual has much further to go but it starts here. It is now the company that generates the revenue and meets its obligations.

It made 'sense' to externalize cost wherever possible, to ensure businesses pay back their loans. Externalizing cost even became the 'reasonable' thing to do. And it makes sense to maximize the income per unit of cost, so it shouldn't be a surprise that management accountancy develops alongside enslavement. Managers required book-keeping to provide information on sugar and cotton plantations, often for owners who were not present and always to increase profits. And so, as Caitlin Rosenthal writes in *Accounting for Slavery*:[28] '[S]lavery became the laboratory for the use of accounting because neat columns of numbers translated more easily to life on plantations than they did to many other early American enterprises.'

Whether society's wider system of accountability picks up the slack arising from this pressure to exclude costs was either not considered, or perhaps was, but nothing was done. There is a difference between financial and social costs and returns, filled by all those 'externalities'. The world will have to wait a while though before anyone notices and even longer before we remember how they occurred. This gap creates risks for society. And as the ability to create financial returns depends on society, these quickly become financial risks, including that specific type of financial risk that has become known as systemic risk. Risks that become so big that if they materialize[29] expected financial returns can no longer cover debt repayment. Risks that a traditional risk register may not address.

Chapter 5

Nineteenth century to 1973

Changes in accountability

In 1833, the UK Government passed the Slavery Abolition Act and paid out £20m in compensation payments[1] to slavers, and nothing to those who had been enslaved. £20m may not seem much today, but this was around 5% of GDP and was the government's biggest payout until the 2008 financial crash. The payments were financed by bonds and loans made by Nathan Rothschild and Moses Montefiore,[2] which UK taxpayers only paid off in 2015. But enslaving people didn't stop in 1833. It declined in British colonies as sugar plantations closed or went bankrupt[3] and international trade restructured, but it continues today, despite the formation of the United Nations and the Universal Declaration of Human Rights in 1948.

This is also an important period for economists, Ricardo, Smith and Marx are all writing during the nineteenth century. Their different perspectives became hardwired into public consciousness, especially Adam Smith's hidden hand, and the mantra of personal economic decision-making being the best way to meet the public interest, and the most effective way of growing the economy. Less commonly shared is his view of land ownership. 'As soon as the land of any country has all become private property, the landlords… love to reap where they never sowed' or 'The interest of the landlord is always opposed to that of the consumer.'[4]

Investing in mining, agriculture, railways and shipping needed a lot more money. Stock exchanges (or public markets) had started as local affairs in coffee houses in the early seventeenth century, with people trading those East India Company shares. Trust ran out with the South Sea Bubble in 1720 though the London Stock Exchange (LSE) wasn't formed in 1801, followed by other exchanges around the country. By 1914 around one-third of global public capital available to investors was traded on the LSE. It is difficult to overstate the contribution of public markets to investment and growth, albeit growth masking costs for which no one would be held to account. A combination of rules and standards for companies listing on exchanges, requirements for accounts – and slowly requirements for audit – were fundamental, replacing personal connections and local knowledge. These new requirements created the trust that meant people could invest in companies where they would never know or meet the managers. This was a huge social innovation in accountability. It wouldn't be until 1973 that LSE would merge with the other British and Irish Exchanges to form a single exchange.[5] New standards, rules and better data opened investment opportunities to an even wider pool of national and international investors.

Stock markets are only half the story and half the money. Some investment came from mobilizing existing capital, but the big money came from lending. Especially if you could lend money that didn't exist but still be paid interest that did. Bank lending started out based on bullion, gold and silver reserves held by a bank. In the UK, the government made it legal for the Bank of England to issue bank notes that were not backed by bullion in the Bank Restriction Act 1797. The pressure was on to make sure those debt repayments and interest payments were coming in, and the chance of accounting recognizing any non-contractual costs in making those returns drifted away into the sunset. And look away politely if anyone mentions usury.[6] The tap had opened.

The Joint Stock Companies Act 1844 established directors rather than shareholders as managers of ordinary business, and directors' responsibilities started to be formalized. In 1854 in *Aberdeen Railway Co v Blaikie Brothers*, the court decided that directors, as agents, had a duty to promote the best interests of the company. As if business owners, debt owners and investors weren't already working hard to ensure their obligations were kept to a minimum, the 1855 Limited

Liability Act set the ball rolling by limiting the liability of investors to their investment. Limited liability created the 'corporate veil', so that creditors can only claim against a company's assets and not the personal assets of shareholders or directors, except in exceptional circumstances, such as fraud. Before 1855, obtaining limited liability needed a separate Act of Parliament, so it would help to be well connected and there were probably fewer than 100 examples between 1800 and 1855. It also required a specific company purpose set out in a clause stating the objects, and there would at least be some discussion in Parliament on how the objects met the public interest before limited liability was awarded.

Obviously, these changes are a good thing it you want to increase private investment, but not a good thing if it makes it harder for anyone experiencing any 'unintended' consequences of that investment to gain redress.[7] In a small part, this risk was offset because a company could not enter into commercial agreements for activities which were outside the objects called acting 'ultra vires', and, by extension, which may not then be in the public interest. But in practice, commercial partners took the risk. In 1875 Ashbury Railway Carriage and Iron Co Ltd entered a contract to finance railway construction abroad, an activity outside its object clause. The House of Lords voided the contract, even though the shareholders had approved it.[8]

All good, but still not enough to unlock the amount of investment needed. Still too much risk. Although organizations had been given rights in law over the years, the separation of owners from the company came quite late. In the United States corporate personhood arose in 1886 from the Supreme Court case *Santa Clara County v Southern Pacific Railroad*. The court found that corporations are 'persons' under the 14th Amendment. In the UK, the critical case was in 1897 in *Salomon v A Salomon & Co Ltd*. The ruling was that a company is a separate legal entity from its owners, which means it has a legal personality and can own property, enter contracts, sue and be sued independently of its shareholders. Transactions relating to contracts can be between a company and other companies or other people. And the company comes between those experiencing consequences and the investors.

There is one more way to avoid obligations and another nail in the coffin for our wider accountability system. Directors have a duty of care to people and to the company they direct, but if a company is now a person, it will also have a duty of care. Well not quite. A company is a legal person but not a biological person, which means its duty of care arises through actions of directors, employees and other agents. It is limited (again!) to reasonable commercial conduct. Which is a shame if we want to go back to the Golden Rule as a basis for that conduct and what is 'reasonable'. It is now much harder to hold the owners of a company to account, especially if the owner is another company, registered in a different jurisdiction.

Governments also need to pay for war, financing this by the sale of government bonds and by increases in taxes, supported by more effort to ensure tax payments are correct. This all helps, as war is big business, and the scale and wider consequences of wars just keep growing. At the beginning of this period, with the Napoleonic Wars, things are bad enough and ever larger armies require widespread voluntary or enforced conscription, and ever more provisioning of arms and materials and logistical support, causing enormous damage to any local populations that they pass through. But nothing was on the scale of the world wars that end this period. Government expenditure was 8% of UK GDP in 1913–14 and over 60% by 1917–18,[9] with the majority spent on military operations. Government used some of this to pay wages of the armed forces, but most was for payments to businesses. Profiteering was rife as wars reduced the scope for a competitive market to drive a 'fair' price. But needs must, and so the question of what level of profit should be paid by the government[10] – and therefore by taxpayers – across contracts for different items a business might be supplying,[11] became a growing concern.

Government tax receipts increase significantly again to finance World War II and stay high to pay for welfare states. But tax is never going to be enough and bonds are the way to go. By 1950s global debt was around 100% of GDP[12] but this was just the beginning. Sovereign and corporate bond borrowing was US$24 trillion in 2024, nearly 25% of the total US$100 trillion indebtedness[13] and the IMF predicted that public debt alone would reach 93% of global GDP.[14] And it is not just public and private sector; add in household debt and the numbers are staggering – US$250 trillion in 2023.[15] These figures exclude the increase in informal and illegal money lending with extremely high interest rates and all that this entails. Debt must be repaid. You might delay paying your suppliers – and many businesses do – and you might be able to tell your investors there won't be a dividend this year. But interest on debt and debt repayments are remorseless. If there is one single pressure on people, as individuals or managers in business, to externalize any costs they can, it is debt.

Though God knows our economic system is very clever at finding new ways to lend more money. Finding new ways to capitalize the commons and shifting resources from common or even public ownership to private ownership doesn't feel like it will help solve society's challenges. With international public and private debt running at these levels, it probably isn't a good idea to find new ways to borrow, or new ways to impose costs on future generations.

Perhaps there is another reason politicians are so hung up about growth. The need for growth so the government can pay back its national debts, especially if repayments were originally predicated on growth. If that debt is not paid back, bad things will happen, and it is in the public interest to avoid those bad things. Which would make the public interest conflicted. We are all in hock to earlier political decisions that favoured current voters over future voters – now in hock to the relatively small number of people who control bond markets. We are trading off a risk of instability from not repaying those debts with a risk of instability from not providing adequate public services. The chickens are coming home to roost.

A nineteenth–twentieth-century externality

If one of the causes of the increase in GDP was enslaving people, the next big contribution to both GDP and externalizing costs came from digging things out of the ground – first coal, then oil and then gas – all made from very old plants. President Ilham Aliyev, talking at the 29th United Nations Climate Change Conference (COP29), stated,

> I said this several months ago, and now those who want to attack me, particularly the international media, simply quote me saying that this is a gift from God. And I want to repeat it here today: it is a gift from God. Every natural resource, whether it's oil, gas, wind, sun, gold, silver, copper, they are all natural resources. Countries should not be blamed for having them and should not be blamed for bringing these resources to the market because the market needs them. The people need them.[16]

The market can be evoked as a way of avoiding any personal or business responsibility. It's what the market wants. Countries should not be blamed for bringing resources to the market, but they could perhaps be blamed for bringing them to markets where there is a difference between private and social costs and returns.

'The people' of course need many things, and they don't get most of them. The people can only have what they want if 'the market' wants to give it to them, as if it has agency. It doesn't. The market is just a place where people, or their agents,[17] come to buy and sell within a set of norms or rules. And the last part is critical. If those norms and rules included the Golden Rule, then the people could only have products or services available in markets that do not damage other people (or themselves).

As with so many of these problems, they are incremental. We get used to them like a frog in water slowly heated to boiling point.[18] Although digging coal out of the ground reached industrial scale in the nineteenth century, coal had been used for heating for a long time. And the potential problems had been noticed for a long time too. We can blame business if we want, or customers, or investors. Or all three. Choose your poison. But the reality is that we are all responding to incentives which have been designed to avoid costs.

Back to all this coal, which, although key to the growth in GDP, came with side effects. Edward I had banned the burning of coal in London in 1272 because of the awful smells. But the shortage of wood meant there was little other option, peat perhaps or dried animal dung. Coal was so much better. It could be picked up from the beach, and London relied mainly on coal from Newcastle beaches, and so the idiom 'carrying coals to Newcastle' comes for any particularly pointless activity. Air quality pollution was, and is, one of the main problems associated with burning coal. In 1661, John Evelyn wrote a pamphlet 'Fumifugium'[19] raising his concerns:

> It is this horrid Smoake which obscures our Churches, and makes our Palaces look old, which fouls our Clothe, and corrupts the Waters, so as the very Rain, and refreshing Dews which fall in the several Seasons, precipitate this impure vapour, which, with its black and tenacious quality, spots and contaminates what forever is expos'd to it.

And Manchester's first Medical Officer of Health, John Leigh, linked poor air quality to the high incidence of respiratory diseases in the city during the 1840s.

Mining has also long been one of the most dangerous occupations, not only from physical injuries and deaths underground but also long term associated health conditions. Early statistics aren't available. But Zola, writing in *Germinal*,[20] about life in a nineteenth-century French mining community, gives us a description, 'The earth was soaked with the black water that oozed from the coal, with the sticky mud along the roads, with the sweat that fell from the exhausted bodies of the miners. In the grey dawn, the settlement slowly emerged, materialising like a vision of poverty.'

Globally, coal mining grew from about 15 million tons in 1800 to 850 million tons in 1900, with the UK making up around 10 million and 250 million tons respectively. By 2000, China was the leading producer on approximately 1.4 billion tons,[21] just ahead of the United States. All this growing pollution means people are experiencing costs that they have not agreed to accept, though the assumption is that the benefits from coal burning outweighed the (unknown) costs. Perhaps the polluter could have paid. In the UK, it took the great smog of London in 1952, which lasted five days, caused 12,000 deaths and untold respiratory illness, before the Clean

Air Act finally came into force in 1956. Some 700 years after Edward I's first attempts. Which brings us to oil, if only in the context of climate change. If the trend in coal was incredible, the trend in oil is steeper and ends at around 4.2 billion tons per year by 2022.[22] And that's before we think about gas.

It is impossible to ignore all this, given how central greenhouse gases have become to global, national and local conversations. Over 50% of carbon emissions come from 36 fossil fuel companies,[23] which risks us jumping to the conclusion that these 36 are the cause. They would contribute zero without their customers. Now the rising temperature is increasing the risk of releasing methane from permafrost and the ocean floor, a greenhouse gas with a significantly higher warming potential than carbon dioxide. While our proposed solutions focus on reducing future fossil fuel use and even setting legal requirements for this, profits continue to be made without recognizing the full costs arising from the use of fossil fuel. Figure 5.1 below shows the consequence. We need investment decisions to respond to price signals that reflect the costs that we are all bearing.

Digging things out of the ground is more than mining. It is also growing things on the land and digging them up every year and becoming more and more 'intensive' about it with consequences for soil health, pollution and flood risk. And where did that land come from?

> In around 1830, Britain had 17 million acres of arable land, 25 million acres of pastureland and fewer than two million acres of forest. But she consumed sugar from the West Indies equivalent (in calories) to the produce of at least another two million acres of wheat, timber from Canada equivalent to another one million acres of woodland, cotton from the Americas equivalent to the wool produced on an astonishing 23 million acres of pastureland, and coal from underground equivalent to 15 million acres of forest. Without these vast 'ghost acres' Britain's industrial revolution, which was only just starting to raise living standards in 1830, would have already shuddered to a halt for lack of calories, cotton or coal.[24]

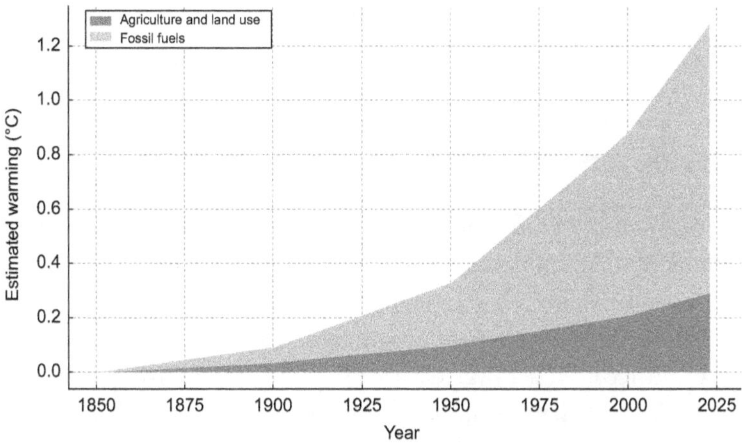

Figure 5.1: Trends in global warming from greenhouse gases by source (1851–2023)

Source: Cumulative contributions to global warming from fossil fuels and agriculture/land use, based on emissions of carbon dioxide (CO_2), methane (CH_4) and nitrous oxide (N_2O). Adapted from Jones et al. (2024), *Our World in Data*, CC BY, ourworldindata.org/grapher/global-warming-by-gas-and-source

Described as ghost acres, profits and future investments were dependent on access to, and subsequent ownership, of all this land.

In the background, society's wider accountability system was being eroded, sharing the cost of some of these non-contractual costs by paying tithes, was in decline. Between the eighteenth and twentieth centuries they had fallen out of use, abolished in Italy as the new state centralized control over the church by 1867, abolished in France during the French Revolution, phased out in Britain by the early twentieth century. Local government and local parishes had to take on this responsibility, raising money through taxes and the Church had to fall back on its own devices. Tax was originally designed as a means of promoting war and paid to the main promoters of those wars, not designed as a means of addressing poverty. No one likes paying either tithes or tax, but we all became a little less accountable for shared, if not individually attributable, obligations.

Developments in financial accounting

The accounting profession really takes off in the nineteenth century with the formation of the first institutes of accountants, and the start of discussions that will end with international accounting standards. The Institute of Chartered Accountants of Scotland (ICAS) was the first and received a Royal Charter in 1854. The ICAEW followed in 1880. Both had an initial focus on protecting suppliers in the event of a business closing, making sure the owners get paid after the suppliers, and reinforcing accounting's focus on contracts and not on the consequences of those contracts. The Institute of Cost and Works Accountants was established a little later in 1919, in response to the growth in interest in cost accounting, largely created by the challenges faced by government procuring so much from arms companies during World War I. In 1916, the Defence of the Realm Act permitted price to be based on a cost of production and a usual rate of profit instead of the market price. Which meant being able to show the cost of production. Costs would have to be recorded against the relevant products or services, and costs that contribute to one of more product or service must be shared across products and services.[25] Cost investigators, combining accountants and engineers would have to check, which led to the rise of cost accounting and management accountancy.

After World War II, the ICAEW and ICAS charters were updated to include references to the public interest. For the ICAEW,

> That it is the belief of the Institute that by reason of the foregoing the furtherance of the objects for which the Institute was originally constituted and incorporated has become increasingly desirable in the public interest and the responsibilities of the Institute have become of greater importance than at the date of the grant of the Original Charter.[26]

For ICAS, 'Societies have found it increasingly necessary in the interests of the public and of their own members that they should act together in promoting the objects which as members of the same profession their respective members entertain in common.' An early chance to consider whether the public were interested in accounts that had a wider scope for which costs should be included was missed.

The biggest boost to the accounting profession is the rise of audit. It is one thing to provide accounting services as required by your customer, and another to provide a service that the law requires businesses to pay for. Public interest created a market and there would be very little audit and a lot less public investment without it. The UK's Joint Stock Companies Act 1844 set the ball rolling by requiring an audit for joint stock companies, and other countries start to follow. The 1900 Companies Act introduces the requirement for external audit, though not that the auditor should be independent or professionally qualified. There is also a requirement for members to get to see a balance sheet, and then in 1907, for this to also be shared with the public through the Registrar of Companies. H. B. Buckley, an authority on company law, said that publishing a balance sheet would be 'the death knell to limited liability'[27] and since the reverse was true, a useful reminder in arguments about additional disclosure. It is not until 1948 that audit must be carried out by independent professionals.

Although we have focused on the UK, the 1929 stock market crash, had a big effect on accounting and accounting standards in the United States, influencing international developments. The Committee on Accounting Procedure was set up in 1939 and audits became required for public companies. The key part of the audit is the audit opinion, and the nature and wording of the opinion has changed over time.[28] Over this period the language has generally referred to whether, in the opinion of the auditor, the accounts provide a true and fair view. And while you may not believe that you have just read a potted history of audit, this last point will prove to be very important.

It is easy to get lost in the technicalities of audit or to ignore it as being the epitome of boredom, but this is to do it an injustice. It is one of the most important social innovations and key in how developments in accounting addresses accountability – to investors but in the public interest. Yes really. It is the push and pull between those preparing financial statements and those auditing those statements that results in financial statements that meet requirements and provide useful information. It underpins public markets and the growth of investment in businesses in those markets.

These improvements also start the drive towards comparability between financial statements and standards for how to produce those statements. Although companies have long been expected to produce accounts, in some shape or size, it wasn't until the Companies Act of 1900 in the UK that companies were legally required to prepare and present financial statements; to keep 'proper books of account' and present a balance sheet to shareholders annually instead of from time to time.

But what are 'proper books of account'? The answer depended on a mix of judicial interpretation in case law and the professional accounting bodies, like the ICAS and the ICAEW. They start to standardize what should be in the accounts including deciding which obligations are unavoidable and which are therefore avoidable. It is meeting a legally enforceable obligation that results in an expense and a cost. No obligation, no cost.

Chapter 6

1973 to now

Changes in accountability

After 1973, the global financial system changed radically as capital controls were largely removed over the 1980s and 1990s. Perhaps 20% of internationally traded companies are trading shares on more than one stock market.[1] GDP and inequality take off and so it shouldn't be a surprise that all the externalities take off as well. Global capital, ownership and management remain dominated by the United States. In 1975, the market capitalization of listed companies globally was just over US$1 trillion with the Dow Jones representing around 60% to 70%. In 2020, market capitalization is US$95.2 trillion, with the US representing 43%.[2] What have become known as the Big Three asset managers[3] – BlackRock, Vanguard and State Street – are the largest or second largest shareholders in more than 98% of S&P 500 firms.[4]

Baby boomers – this has all happened on our watch – and we have trained the next generation to do the same. There is no point blaming the past, but after 1973 we had the techniques to account for externalities, and we could probably have avoided most of the current crises. Professor John Ruggie, who served as the UN Secretary-General's Special Representative on Business and Human Rights, in a report to the UN Human Rights Council in 2008[5] said 'the root cause of the business and human rights predicament… lies in the governance gaps created by globalization'. Exactly. While the economic, political and social power of corporations has increased, the capacity for 'societies to manage their adverse consequences'[6] has not kept pace. The transnational character and legal structure of corporations make these governance gaps much worse, along with the proliferation of bilateral investment treaties and the liberalization of trade. These all make it more difficult to hold corporations accountable for violations of human rights. States are considered the primary duty-bearer for human rights and accessing justice for victims of corporate human rights abuse becomes extremely difficult.

While we have been focusing on new examples of the costs imposed on people but for which those responsible are not held to account, all the other externalized costs carry on racking up; climate change, nature loss and unpaid labour. Recognizing that businesses, and business profits, have been dependent on unpaid women's labour doesn't mean it stops. Even though women have become consumers, providing new markets, this dependency continues, moving further down global supply chains to other women who pay these costs, who accept low incomes to survive, under social and cultural structures which reduce their freedom and their choices. These are also externalities, resulting in a mismatch between private and societal returns, legitimized by accounting practice.

Twentieth–twenty-first-century externalities

The big one is now the 'externality' being experienced by future generations. This has always been there, but the scale of private and public debt makes the consequences hard to ignore. But none of the others have gone away. We had to wait until 1975 for the first UN World Conference on Women, held in Mexico City. The UN Decade for Women followed in 1976, and the Convention on the Elimination of All Forms of Discrimination Against Women was adopted by the UN in 1979 with the Beijing Declaration and Platform for Action in 1995. Before we get carried away, we could be talking about a different world. Figure 6.1 below shows the trend in the global gender gap. Not much has changed since the first report in 2006. At current rates we still need around 123 years to close the gender equality gap.[7] Estimates vary but surely anything over a week or so must be unacceptable.

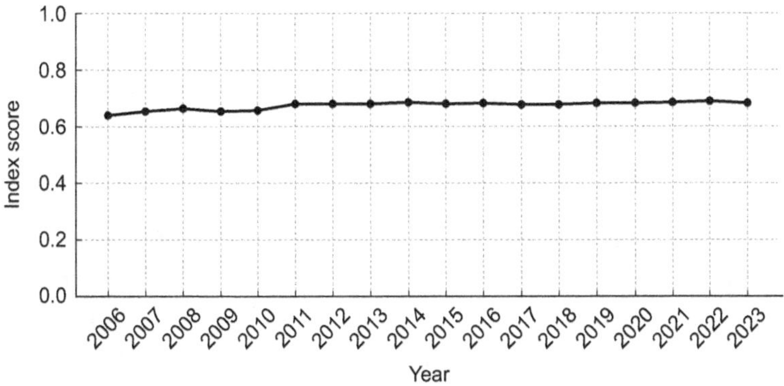

Figure 6.1: Global gender gap index (2006–2023)

Source: Figure based on data from the World Economic Forum, Global Gender Gap Reports (2006–2023), available at www.weforum.org.

Despite progress in many areas as emphasized in the 2025 UNICEF report on adolescent girls' rights over 30 years, there is still so much to do.

> Worldwide, about one in three adolescent girls and boys aged 15–19 consider a husband to be justified in hitting his wife under at least one of the following circumstances: if she burns the food, argues with him, goes out without telling him, neglects the children or refuses sexual relations.[8]

A World Health Organization report found that 27% of women aged between 15 and 49 have experienced physical or sexual violence by an intimate partner.[9] Back to Silvia Federici, 'Once again much of the violence unleashed is directed against women, for in the age of the computer, the conquest of the female body is still a precondition for the accumulation of labour and wealth…'[10] In July 2024, in the UK, the National Police Chief's Council declared that violence against women and girls was a national emergency.

While there have been some advances in some parts of the world, women still generally provide household labour, labour that often includes roles that extend beyond the household, for example, weeding on small holder farms and caring for children and the elderly. Most of the goods and services we pay for depend on this unpaid labour throughout their supply chains. This is pervasive even in the glittering world of the internet, AI and social media. As Phil Jones explains in *Work Without the Worker*,[11]

> [A] woman living in Kenya's Dadaab, among the world's largest refugee camps, wanders across the vast dusty site to a central hut lined with computers. Like many others who have been brutally displaced and then warehoused at the margins of our global system, her days are spent toiling away for a new capitalist vanguard thousands of miles away in Silicon Valley. A day's work might include labelling videos, transcribing audit or showing algorithms how to identify various photos of cats. Amid a drought for real employment, clickwork represents one of the few 'formal' options for Dadaab's residents, though the work is volatile, arduous and, when waged, paid by the piece.

Jones[12] also reported that 'Micro' employment is growing. Zero hours contracts or intense competition for 15 minute 'contracts', excluding any of the costs that were once taken as a sign of progress, like paid holidays or health insurance. A long way away from ILO conventions, especially in the digital economy where people are finding, competing for and delivering short term contracts for work taking only a couple of minutes for an anonymous employer. And self-employment may be a route to riches for some, but for many it is a route to lower salaries, longer hours and whole lot of worry.

Meanwhile slavery has a new name: Modern-day slavery. The global approach to minimizing the cost of labour has become more subtle. Zero hours contracts may be an issue in richer countries but the scale of underemployment, hardly any payment, or no payment at all, is hard to conceive and is in all those global supply chains. And the flow of resources hasn't stopped either. Research in 2017[13] found that sub-Saharan Africa received US$161 billion from loans, remittances and aid, but US$203 billion left the continent, some direct through trade, some through tax management, some through investment returns. Where the owners of the investments are in the Global North, investing in the Global South, there will be a net financial flow from south to north, even with impact investment, where a net financial flow is offset by the 'impact'.[14]

The International Labour Organization (ILO) estimates that more than 40 million people are subjected to modern slavery,[15] encompassing forced labour, forced sexual exploitation and forced marriages. None of which makes for comfortable reading.[16] It is also increasingly hard to draw a line between a fair and voluntary contract and a 'take any work you can get to survive' contract. SDG 8 covers decent work and economic growth but according to the UN's 2023 SDG report,[17] progress is patchy to say the least:

> The situation was most alarming in [Less Developed Countries (LDC)], where informal employment stood at 89.7 per cent in 2022, with no improvement since 2015. Sub-Saharan Africa and Central and Southern Asia also continued to have high informality rates, at 87.2 per cent and 84.8 per cent, respectively. Women have been worse off during the employment recovery, with four out of five jobs created in 2022 for women being informal, compared to only two out of three jobs for men.

The drive and ability to externalize cost is as relentless as our inability to stop buying things that come with so much harm. So much for 'do unto others as you would do unto yourself'. It is hardly our fault that the global system of accountability is failing to hold fourth tier suppliers to account. In case you were sighing in relief at that point, it is our fault. We buy the products.

And the commons continue to decline. Or, as we might more accurately describe this, the process of land grabbing. Land grabbing has increased rapidly since 2000, widening inequality and undermining people's lives[18] with Indigenous people being mainly affected in an ongoing history of the loss of their land.[19] Between 2006 and 2012, more than 400 large-scale land acquisitions have been recorded, covering nearly 35 million hectares across 66 countries mainly in the

Global South.[20] And these are just the ones led by foreign investors for production of food crops.

If you read one reference from this book, read *Caliban and the Witch* by Silvia Federici. Silvia's analysis is that:

> It is in this context that a feminist perspective on the commons is important because it begins with the realization that, as the primary subjects of reproductive work, historically and in our time, women have depended on access to communal natural resources more than men and have been most penalized by their privatization and most committed to their defence.[21]

For some, land transfer will be seen as a good thing. In a simple example of the tragedy of the commons,[22] herders over graze commonly owned pasture and the solution is for the herders to individually own parts of the commons. Any management of a resource, with or without forms of ownership, comes with limits and responsibilities whether individual, in partnership, in common or by local or national government. And all depend on effective maintenance of limits and enforcement of responsibilities. Even where land is owned in trust, it is passing to private ownership. Not to manage it more efficiently but because of pressure on provision of public services. In *The New Enclosure: The Appropriation of Public Land in Neoliberal Britain*, Brett Christophers presented data to show that around 10% of the United Kingdom's land area had been transferred from public to private ownership over a 40-year period. And all because the calculation of profit from the sale of that land did not account for any costs arising from the loss of common ownership.

There is one more externality to consider. Nature. Of course, there were impacts and dependencies on nature in earlier periods, but the scale has ramped up and finally there is an increasing realization that life as we know it depends on nature – of which, to be clear, human beings form a part.

After watching any equivalent to the UK's Sir Richard Attenborough, it is hard to know where to start to describe the scale of damage. What follows here is very short and very selective and, depressingly quickly, out-of-date summary. The purpose is only to emphasize the same point, that an accounting system that allows costs caused by a business to be excluded from resource allocation decisions will be destructive. For some of those resources, an appropriate cost might be so high, or at least so unknown, as to make the resource unusable unless we want to risk doing more harm than good. Deep-sea mining would be an example. If the potential cost is too high, it is no longer a resource to be used, it is just part of our world. The relentless drive to commodify (and sell things and borrow money to do so) exerts relentless pressure to minimize or avoid costs wherever possible. And the accounting system allows investors, or their agents, to ignore these costs and, by default, make it all acceptable.

Around three-quarters of the world's flowering plants and one-third of global food crops need to be pollinated by insects, predominantly bees.[23] With the decline in pollinators from climate change, loss of habitat and pesticides (especially neonicotinoids), pollination and food production is declining globally, by 3% to 5% in one year according to one study.[24] Declining production brings significant economic and human consequences, an estimated 427,000 additional human deaths in one year. One solution has been to ship in bees. In 2021, 2.6 million colonies pollinated the almond crop in California alone,[25] but the use of managed bees is not offsetting the drop in pollination by (free) wild bees. According to another study in 2019,[26] more than 40% of insect species are declining and a third are endangered. But studies and reports on the decline of insects, whether it is butterflies or dung beetles, are now common. It has been described as the sixth mass extinction. Fewer insects mean less food, and fewer fish and fewer birds will have significant effects on ecosystems on which human beings depend. The Food and Agriculture Organization (FAO)'s research[27] shows that fish stocks are falling, from 90% within biologically sustainable levels in 1974 to 62% in 2021. Palm oil production has gone from 2 million to 80 million tons between 1970 and 2020[28] and now uses 30 million hectares of land. Much of this used to be rain forest, swapping from converting a diverse ecosystem supporting many animals and plants to a monoculture supporting very few and a release of carbon dioxide. And then there are plastics. Again, so many issues, especially with microplastics, which are reducing plants' ability to photosynthesize[29] and a US$1.5 trillion cost for health-related damages.[30]

And so on. Between 1970 and 2017, 2.5 trillion tons of materials were extracted, with high and upper middle-income countries being the main beneficiaries.[31] According to the United Nations Environment Programme (UNEP),[32] this resource extraction has nearly tripled and is the main cause of biodiversity loss and water stress. All driven by inequality as richer countries can export extinction. Enough numbers. None of this is good. Well, of course, the products and services that have been produced have been useful to consumers, have often resulted in lower cost foods than alternatives. But had these other costs, hidden in supply chains,[33] been factored in, either those benefits may not justify the cost, or the products and services might have had to have been adapted. We may have made different choices, created different products and services, and life may have been different. The trend in externalities is going to be similar to the trend in GDP, but unlike GDP where much of the increase has been in the Global North, much of the increase in externalities has been in the Global South.

Finally, there are some signs that international legislation is catching up. In May 2025, the Inter-American Court of Human Rights issued an advisory opinion on 'the Climate Emergency and Human Rights'[34] recognizing the human right to a healthy environment as an autonomous right. Citizens can directly claim that their right to a healthy environment is being violated. In July 2025, the International Court of Justice also gave its advisory opinion on 'the Obligations of States in respect of Climate Change',[35] which included a duty for States to:

> prevent significant harm to the environment by acting with due diligence and to use all means at their disposal to prevent activities carried out within their jurisdiction or control from causing significant harm to the climate system and

> other parts of the environment, in accordance with their common but differentiated responsibilities and respective capabilities.

These are encouraging signs but without externalities being included in the calculation of profit, investment will flow to activities that generate externalities faster than the legal system can keep up.

Chapter 7

Financial accounting, 1973 to date

This is the period when accounting, both the profession and standards, really take-off and nail down which costs should be accounted for. It needs its own chapter. As globalization increased and the profession grew, standardization had to be a good thing. And since World War II, the profession had sought to standardize accounting practices, because they make financial reports comparable. The profession was led by the US, UK, Australia and Canada, reflecting the interests and power of those countries.

Although it is now accepted that the IFRS Foundation, overseeing the IASB, and the FAF, overseeing the FASB, are the recognized bodies for issuing accounting standards, there is nothing to stop a country issuing its own standards. In fact, many base their accounting standards on the IASB standards but add and subtract as required. In the UK the applicable accounting standards are the Financial Reporting Standards (FRS). In Canada, it is the Accounting Standards for Private Enterprises (ASPE), India has its Indian Accounting Standards, and so on.

The way in which standards were developed to decide which obligations should be included in the accounts continued to focus primarily on obligations arising from contracts. Other costs, imposed on people who are not party to those contracts, are not generally included and so they become externalities. They become referred to as social or environmental issues, or sustainability issues, language that is then used for the effects of the business as well as effects on the business. It is an example of how language can evolve to create a distance from reality, describing examples of imposing costs on other people, or abusing their human rights as 'sustainability issues', or even, 'sustainability-related financial disclosures'.

Our economic system could have gone a very different way and at a few points it nearly did. It was closer than we might think.

In case you were wondering, this and the last chapter start in 1973 because this is the year that the International Accounting Standards Committee (IASC) is formed to address a growing demand for more standardization.[1] It was chaired by Sir Henry Benson, the senior partner of Coopers & Lybrand,[2] and president of the ICAEW between 1966–67. And it was by no means a given that the IASC, and later the IFRS Foundation, would be accepted as the right place for oversight and governance of those standards. After all, the initial membership wasn't all that representative. The IASC was an independent private-sector organization that sought 'to achieve uniformity in the accounting principles that are used by businesses and other organisations for financial reporting around the world'.[3] Their goal was to 'formulate and publish in the public interest accounting standards to be observed in the presentation of financial statements and to promote their worldwide acceptance'.

The countries involved were Australia, Canada, France, Germany, Ireland, Japan, Mexico, the Netherlands, the United Kingdom and the United States. Between 1976 and 1985 the Chairs and Secretaries were from Australia, Canada, the United Kingdom or the United States,[4] which just might have imparted some bias. There were also more common law countries involved which may have contributed to a principles-based approach. Membership was from the accounting bodies of those countries, as opposed to government representatives, further ensuring the focus is on standardizing accounting practice, rather than on considering what the public interest should be behind those standards. And membership was entirely male which might just have imparted a bit more bias.

The IASC approved the first international accounting standard, 'International Accounting Standard (IAS) 1 Disclosure of Accounting Policies', in 1974 and it was published in 1975. This is only 51 years ago. International standards are a very recent phenomenon compared to our starting point in the eleventh century, and the culmination of the story of unaccounted for costs imposed on others. Just how close we came to spotting the problem can be seen in the work of the American Institute of Certified Public Accountants (AICPA)'s Study Group (all-male) on the Objectives of Financial Statements.[5] Not surprisingly this group was in the 'the only thing investors are interested in is personal financial returns' camp. It starts well and they get so close, but this became an exercise in missed opportunities, reliant on some critical assumptions. It is worth looking at some of these to see just what might have been. It may bring a tear to the eye.

> Users' needs for information, however, are not known with any degree of certainty. No study has been able to identify precisely the specific role financial statements play in the economic decision-making process. This Study is therefore dependent upon certain assumptions about users' information needs and their decision processes. These assumptions are supported by research available to the Study Group and are believed to be consistent with economic and behavioural theory.[6]
>
> In the United States, where the economic system emphasizes private enterprise, individuals and enterprises generally attempt to maximize their own wealth.[7]
>
> The Study Group prefers the development of financial statement objectives by a professional, as distinguished from a political, process.[8]
>
> All commercial enterprises and, in fact, all individuals and groups use resources provided by society, and they pay for them through taxes and other government levies.[9]
>
> … because our social and economic system assumes that the pursuit of private goals generally tends to fulfil the social ones.[10]

So much depends on an assumption about the purpose, as the basis for decision-useful information for users, with very little actual discussion or research with those users.[11] All this, despite an earlier statement that they don't want to be political as if a *professional* process is detached from politics, and despite a statement that recognizes dependency on resources provided by society, and the assumption that those resources are paid for 'through taxes' and paid for at their replacement cost.

And yet there was hope.

'An equally difficult reporting problem arises when an enterprise's activities *impose a cost on society*. The notions of accountability and corporate responsibility imply the need for *disclosure of the consequences of such activities*; but identifying, measuring and reporting their consequences without standards and guidelines is troublesome. Only society through laws and regulation can identify what it considers a cost or sacrifice. And only society can determine the extent to which it will absorb such costs or force enterprises either to modify their activities to eliminate social 'costs or else to pay for them. *In these ways, social costs become private monetary costs that affect enterprise earnings and earning power*'[12] (emphasis added).

If you have reached this point and are still concerned that the arguments about the exclusion of costs seem a long way from what accounting is designed to do, read this again. The quote is basically a restatement of the accountability framework at the start of Part 2 of this book, sadly, adding the assumption that measurement is too troublesome to result in useful information. It is fundamental. Yes, it is surely only government that can identify these costs and the processes by which they can be accounted for, and not a study group or even the IASC. At this point they might have said 'we can't do this alone; we need representatives of society, of those incurring costs, in this discussion' but instead a group of, presumably, middle-class male accountants took it on themselves. They did recognize that society could make enterprises pay the costs they impose on society and, had those other people been in the room, they might together have explored how accounting standards could be applied to do just that – in the public interest. They came so close.

'An objective of financial statements is to report on those activities of the enterprise affecting society which can be determined and described or measured and which are important to the role of the enterprise in its social environment.'[13]

How did this get left out of the IFRS Conceptual Framework?[14] Understandably perhaps as a series of standards were being developed to address specific accounting issues. IAS1 covers presentation of financial statements, IAS2 covers inventories and so on, up to IAS41 for agriculture. There wasn't a document that pulled these together and set out the users, their decisions and what their expectations were thought to be until IASC produced the Framework for Preparation and Presentation of Financial Statements in 1989.[15] Plenty of time to miss something out that would address how an enterprise affects society.

Despite all this work, at least in the UK, accounting was facing challenges and users were losing confidence. The Accounting Standards Board (ASB) was established to address these challenges, chaired by David Tweedie. He co-wrote a history of this period and the preface starts, 'In the late 1980s, financial accounting in Britain was in disarray.'[16] It is hard now to look back and realize the challenge of restoring honesty and trust in accounting, in part by developing standards, in the face of resistance from across the financial sector which was still able to influence reporting of profits. In 1999, the ASB produced a Statement of Principles for Financial Reporting that reaffirmed that the users included Government.

> Governments and their agencies are interested in the allocation of resources and, therefore, the activities of entities. They also require information that assists them in regulating the activities of entities, assessing taxation and providing a basis for national statistics.

The IASC handed over its standard setting role to the IASB on 1 April 2001.[17] The IASB adopted the IASC's conceptual framework and updated it in 2010, including chapters on the Objective of General Purpose Financial Reporting and on Qualitative Characteristics of Useful Financial Information. In 2018 the concept of stewardship and management's performance as a steward of a business's economic resources is fully introduced. Unfortunately, the primary users are reduced to existing and potential investors, providers of loan finance and other creditors. You can see how this would seem reasonable from one perspective as those are the three main groups on the credit side of the accounts, and all have a call on the assets of a company. Government has gone from the list of users although would still be included under 'other creditors', since there are going to be outstanding tax bills. So, all seems OK. Except that when we look at the interest of those primary users, it will not be OK at all.

What was the discussion that supported this fundamental shift? We have minutes of a meeting in 2008 taken by the Financial Accounting Standards Board (FASB),[18] who attended the IASB meetings where the issue was discussed, with support for providers of capital as being the primary user though with some dissent. And a report of a meeting where this was discussed in 2009,[19] which says there was broad support for a primary user group. But little recorded on the pros and cons of who would be in the group.

The problem is in the exposure draft of the chapter on the Objective of General Purpose Financial Reporting in paragraph OB2,

> to provide financial information about the reporting entity[20] that is useful to present and potential equity investors, lenders and other creditors in making decisions in their capacity as capital providers. Information that is decision-useful to capital providers may also be useful to other users of financial reporting who are not capital providers.[21]

Capital providers' interest was defined in paragraph OB9,

> Capital providers are interested in financial reporting because it provides information that is useful for making decisions. The decisions that capital providers make include whether and how to allocate their resources to a particular entity (i.e. whether and how to provide capital) and whether and how to protect or enhance their investments. When making those decisions, capital providers are interested in assessing the entity's ability to generate net cash inflows and management's ability to protect and enhance the capital providers' investments.

The loss of government as a primary user receiving tax payments is particularly painful. Government's interest is not primarily as a capital provider. It is primarily as a recipient of tax payments and the purpose of those tax payments is for the well-being of residents, citizens and service users, the point made clear in the IPSASB Conceptual Framework.[22] Though this was not published until 2014. If government was still a user, not hidden in 'other creditors', it would be obvious that the expectation of users could not be limited to financial returns but is also to maintain and enhance the well-being of citizens, residents and services users.[23] There is no point in the government receiving tax revenues if it spends them clearing up problems generated by the companies that pay the tax. In his report for the Food Farming and Countryside Commission on the food industry.[24] Professor Tim Jackson concluded that the food-related cost of chronic disease caused by the food ecosystem in the UK is £268 billion a year. The direct cash element of this in health, social care and welfare costs of £99.1 billion. The total amount of corporation tax from all businesses in 2023/4 was £93.3 billion.[25] Every pound had to be spent dealing with the costs created by the food industry. Of course, businesses in this industry also employ people and their employees also pay income tax and then buy things generating VAT, so government total income from taxes is higher. But in 2021 the profits of the biggest eight ultra processed food companies were £23 billion.[26] Even a 50% tax wouldn't go far towards addressing the costs. And then health care costs become payments to pharma companies and so the not-so-merry-go-round goes around.

Imagine what the food industry would look like if the companies involved had to account for an estimate of their share of these costs, where a good enough estimate was one that reflected the public interest. In any case it is hard for governments to intervene against the lobbying pressure of commercial interests.[27] Unless of course, the government was a user of the financial reports and its interests in the wider costs of business meant these costs had to be included in the accounts.

Meanwhile the increase in the size of the welfare state and public sector activity meant there was an increasing need for accountants working in the public sector. In 1986 the IFAC established the Public Sector Committee (PSC) to enhance public financial management and accountability. In 1996, the PSC shifted its focus to developing international accounting standards. In 2004, it was restructured and rebranded as the International Public Sector Accounting Standards Board (IPSASB), reflecting its mandate to develop and issue international public sector accounting standards.

There were other organizations that had the potential to take up the mantle of accounting standards. The UN was one alternative and had established the Ad hoc Inter-Governmental Working Group on accounting standards and reporting in 1979. The OECD was another option with its own study group. The IASC had to work hard to maintain its autonomy and gain acceptance to be able to set international accounting standards, particularly acceptance by the IOSCO. Sir Henry Benson, writing in the *Financial Times* in 1978, was concerned with the danger arising from the presence in the UN of several countries including communist republics,[28] and other countries raised concerns about the Anglo-Saxon dominance of the Committee. There were many options for governance, for purpose and for standards. But the opportunity to reconsider the purpose of accounting at that time had passed.

Alongside all these developments, accounting standards also consider the nature of expenditure arising from an obligation. The IASC established a steering committee on liabilities, starting in 1984, as building blocks in developing a conceptual framework. But an obligation was not defined by the FASB until 1985 in 'Statement of Financial Accounting Concepts No. 6' and, by the IFRS Foundation, in the 1989 Conceptual Framework. In the current 2001 version of IAS 37, currently being updated, it has become a bit more complex. Most of the definition from paragraph 10, going to the heart of which costs are now accounted for, is below. It is critical.

> A liability is a present obligation of the entity arising from past events, the settlement of which is expected to result in an outflow from the entity of resources embodying economic benefits.

> An obligating event is an event that creates a legal or constructive obligation that results in an entity having no realistic alternative to settling that obligation.
>
> A legal obligation is an obligation that derives from: (a) a contract (through its explicit or implicit terms); (b) legislation; or (c) other operation of law.
>
> A constructive obligation is an obligation that derives from an entity's actions where:
>
> (a) by an established pattern of past practice, published policies or a sufficiently specific current statement, the entity has indicated to other parties that it will accept certain responsibilities; and
> (b) as a result, the entity has created a valid expectation on the part of those other parties that it will discharge those responsibilities.

The IFRS only become a legal requirement following voluntary adoption by national governments and regulators. Which will take us back to the public interest. And although the public interest might expect a higher level of responsibility and obligation than the embodiment of all these years of accounting practice, governments have generally signed up. Just perhaps without considering the alternatives. If anything, the IFRS Foundation's launch of the ISSB may increase a risk of understanding sustainability within the needs of capital markets,[29] rather than understanding capital markets within the needs of sustainability.

Countries that were colonies have gained their freedom, sometimes even without a war. Freeing themselves from oppression, they stuck with the system of international accounting which legitimized the extraction of value from their countries. This may seem extraordinary but then we have all gone along with an accounting system that extracts value. It is also less extraordinary if you need to borrow money from the IMF and the World Bank and want to attract inward investment from multinationals. While countries kicked out their colonial oppressors, they mainly kept the same Companies

Acts, with the same requirement for company accounts, almost as if the underpinning philosophy must be aligned with their own culture and their own history.

It might seem surprising that financial reporting has managed to achieve such a level of international consistency, until realizing that for countries seeking international investment or businesses wanting to join global supply chains, standardization was an implicit requirement by regulators of capital markets. National company legislation generally refers to using applicable accounting standards, in practice this means international standards or close to them. In a global economy it just wasn't going to be possible, or at least not easy, for a country to use its own radically different standards.

Those concerned about the sole focus on financial returns could have argued against these developments and sought to change it to something more holistic. But as the IFRS Foundation and the IASB had boxed off accounting standards, made them appear very boring, added many layers to structures and governance and described them in terms of economic phenomena, it is perhaps also not surprising what happened next. Those with concerns got busy with non-financial reporting standards, standards that addressed social and environmental issues. Sometime later, realizing that these were somewhat divorced from the economic system and not actually influencing resource allocation decisions or addressing the now increasing challenges, work started on integrated reporting. The International Integrated Reporting Council launched a framework in 2021,[30] which should perhaps have required accounting to have an integrated purpose that was more than only financial returns.

And all these challenges led to a profusion of other approaches. Many focused on new business models as the solution. Cooperatives have been around for as long as private limited companies, but international interest in, and examples of social enterprises, grew rapidly,[31] with varying success but more focus on ownership than reporting. Doughnut Economics positioned economics within social and environmental boundaries with governance and ownership implications for business.[32] Other approaches focused on transforming existing business models.

Sadly, the same level of consistency, or a focus on a defined primary user group, that has been achieved in financial reporting, didn't follow. This could have meant focusing on people experiencing consequences and understanding their needs and expectations in designing useful information, rather than 'sustainability issues'. The Global Reporting Initiative (GRI) was launched in 1997 to standardize reporting on environmental, social and economic impacts, and has been followed by many others. A Taskforce for Climate-related Financial Disclosures (TCFD) was followed by a Taskforce for Nature-related Financial Disclosures (TNFD) and then a Taskforce on Social and Inequality and Social-related Financial Disclosures (TISFD). There are increasing numbers of legislative changes – such as the European Union's Corporate Sustainability Reporting Directive (CSRD)[33] and the Corporate Sustainability Due Diligence Directive (CSDDD).[34]

There is also growing interest in how positive impacts and reduced dependencies on other capitals (nature, social, human and produced) might be accounted for, included in capital accounts and, where appropriate, recognized as assets[35] under existing accounting standards.[36] So long as the transactions and related contracts address negative externalities, this will improve investors' understanding of the value of other capitals and encourage businesses to create long-term value, incentivizing a shift to regenerative and more equitable investment.

At the same time there were international developments covering public, private and civil society. The Millennium Development Goals were launched in 2000, followed by the Sustainable Development Goals in 2015. After the Rio Summit in 1992, the United Nations Framework Convention on Climate Change (UNFCCC)'s first COP (Conferences of the Parties to UN environmental treaty frameworks)[37] was in 1995, leading to the Kyoto Protocol in 1997. Some 29 COPs later,[38] the implications for the way profit is calculated compared to international agreements is clear. Climate targets risk not being met and global average temperature increased by over 1.5% in 2024.[39] And that's just SDG 13 Climate Action, a topic on which the Paris Agreement had been adopted in 2015. It's a similar story for other SDGs. According to the UN's 2023 progress report, 30% of the targets showed no progress or had regressed. For SDG 5 Gender Equality,

> At the current rate, it will take an estimated 300 years to end child marriage, 286 years to close gaps in legal protection and remove discriminatory laws, 140 years for women to be represented equally in positions of power and leadership in the workplace, and 47 years to achieve equal representation in national parliaments.[40]

The report didn't reflect on when costs arising from gender equality would be reflected in international accounting standards.

The focus of many of these initiatives is still information for the same user and same purpose as financial reporting but even where it is not, the information is in a separate report and the approach to calculating profit remains unchanged, bar perhaps the occasional write down of asset values. The key problem, that costs are not being accounted for in the calculation of profit, still needs to be addressed. The rate at which voluntary or even mandatory sustainability reporting standards are going to reduce the negative consequences will always be lower than the rate at which those decisions create negative consequences. At some point in the future, ESG could come to be seen as the twenty-first century's version of bloodletting: always prescribed, mainly harmless – except where it has drawn attention away from the problem of profit calculation. But it has provided accountants and auditors with lots to do and auditing (and advisory) services increase even as the minimum size of company that must have an audit has continued to drift upwards.

It is not until 1976 that the Consultative Committee of Accountancy Bodies established an Auditing Practices Committee and not until 1991 that the Auditing Practices Board was established and started to replace Audit Practice Notes with Statements of Auditing Standards.[41] One small, but critical, change is the audit opinion, which may be hard to believe. Companies of all types, generally over a certain size, relating to turnover, balance sheet value or employment, are audited. In the UK, the Companies Act of 1981 required financial statements to conform with applicable accounting principles as well as give a true and fair view. And from the Companies Act 1985, financial statements also had to be prepared in accordance with the requirements of the Act, slowly adding on from an opinion on whether the accounts are true and fair, which leads to a typical modern opinion that says:

> 'In our opinion the accounts:
> - give a true and fair view of the financial position;
> - have been properly prepared in accordance with accounting standards (e.g., FRS 102 or IFRS); and
> - are compliant with the Companies Act 2006.'

These are three separate opinions. And as the law makes clear, preparation in accordance with accounting standards does not mean that the accounts give a true and fair view. Despite this, there may be a risk. If you think that your accounts are in accordance with accounting standards, surely they will also give a true and fair view and will comply with the Companies Act 2006? Buy one get two free. As we will see in Chapter 9, this is not necessarily the case.

Alongside financial accounting for organizations, approaches to national accounting have also been developing. The System of Environmental-Economic Accounting (SEEA)[42] uses accounting approaches to integrate data on the elements of well-being and sustainability, to deal with what gets left out of GDP. These additional accounts encompass topics such as health care, education and training, unpaid household service work, household distributional accounts for income, consumption and wealth, labour accounts and accounts for human capital. The SEEA-based data are under development in over 90 countries which feeds into the System of National Accounts (SNA). The SNA[43] is supported by the UN Statistics Division and provides a standard set of recommendations for measuring economic activity – in other words, GDP. The SNA was updated in early 2025 and includes new chapters on the measurement of well-being and sustainability and provides a focal point for the further development and integration of accounting-based approaches to the organization of data. A single indicator to replace GDP is not envisaged but through the progressive linking of a wider range of data, there is a clear potential to establish comparable data sets across aspects of well-being and sustainability.

This international framework provides a context for the growing number of national approaches to well-being accounting. Many governments have recognized the limitations of using GDP as the basis for measuring 'success' and formulating policy and are looking at how to move towards well-being and using measures of well-being alongside GDP. The OECD's Report for the G7 Finance Ministers and Central Bank Governors includes a detailed summary of legislative and other embedding mechanisms including support for indicators for measuring welfare.[44] The Welsh Government's Well-Being of Future Generations Act 2015[45] requires public bodies to consider the well-being of future generations and includes seven well-being goals that public bodies must work towards. This has meant that Audit Wales,[46] the statutory external auditor of most of the Welsh public sector, has had to develop approaches to assess performance against this requirement.[47] Audit Wales and the Future Generation's Commissioner produced their first reports on progress in 2020.

In 2019, the New Zealand Government developed a national well-being budget.[48] The well-being objectives take an intergenerational view and focus on ensuring that well-being is the basis of investment decisions. The Australian Government has launched a national well-being framework 'Measuring What Matters,'[49] to inform government decision making with inclusion, equity and fairness as cross-cutting dimensions. OECD's well-being framework[50] is a well-established approach for measuring people's well-being. OECD continue to develop work through the Centre on Well-being, Inclusion, Sustainability and Equal Opportunity (WISE),[51] which was established in 2020.

There is now a growing body of practice on how organizations can account for well-being and several international standards referring to well-being. As well as the 'International Organization for Standardization (ISO) 37005, Governance of Organizations – Developing Indicators for Effective Governance',[52] a British Standard,

'PAS 808, Purpose led organisations',[53] makes well-being the fundamental purpose and is now the basis for a new international standard, ISO 37011. All these are based on the definition of well-being used in another British Standard, 'BS 8950 Understanding and Enhancing Social Value',[54] that well-being 'captures states of being where subjective and objective psychological or physical human needs are met in varying degrees, with increased well-being corresponding with better states of physical and psychological health'. And there are increasing arguments for post-growth[55] economies and other research on how well-being can be increased without economic growth.[56]

The United Nations Development Programme's (UNDP) SDG Impact Standards are also the basis for a joint UNDP/ISO Standard on SDG Management, ISO 53001/2.[57] Over the last 15 years, SVI has been developing and supporting an international community of people, across over 50 countries, developing standards of practice[58] for accounting for well-being. The Capitals Coalition has developed protocols for stand-alone[59] and integrated[60] assessment of impacts and dependencies on natural, social and human capitals.

Conclusion to Part 2

It is easy to understand how society's initially imperfect approach to holding all of us to account for our actions has developed in a way that has widened the gaps, allowing more people, those with power, to become less accountable for their actions. It is also easy to understand how financial accounting has developed over time to reflect that power imbalance, to focus on what can most easily be accounted for, from the perspective of the direct users of accounts. And not with those indirectly affected by a business operations, creating a widening gap between public and private interest. Up to a point.

From 1973 onwards, it would have been possible to reverse this. It would have been possible for those producing accounting standards to realize they were not able to represent the public interest without wider stakeholder input. It would have been possible for those developing the regulations within which accounting standards are used to realize the gap was widening. It might even have been possible to bring the operation of the accounting system under an international treaty. None of this happened; conflicts of interest, vested interests and the liberalization of the world economy made it much less likely.

If, from the start, financial forecasts had to include costs for expected harm, there probably wouldn't have been that shift in the distribution of global GDP. Some of today's business models wouldn't have made it past the bank manager's door. Imagine restating all those early accounts of coal mines or cigarette companies to include all these costs. It is not markets that did this; it is the social expectations of what costs are included in the calculation of profit. Human creativity and imagination being what they are, there would have been different business models providing goods and services that did not, by definition, come with all those costs. If the accounting system had developed with a stronger link between public and private accounting, and government had remained a user of both, perhaps it would have been more integrated around ideas of well-being.

It is always dangerous to predict an end. Capitalism, the set of behaviours that arise from a failure of accountability and resulting rules, standards and norms, has proved extraordinarily resilient. It has constantly found new markets, across time and space. More is always better. More is necessary. So many people with not enough to survive, over 700 million people going to bed hungry each and every day.[1] Do those of us who have so much, really need more stuff? You can always borrow against your future income, so you can have more stuff right now. Stuff that you only use occasionally, at weekends or on holiday. If you have no more space, you can go online and find a virtual space somewhere where you can buy virtual stuff, and the turnover of stuff is also going up. The rate at which we buy and dispose of our clothes has gone through the roof. Hopefully we are all much happier, spending lots of time thinking about stuff. More stuff. But only one world. It feels like a giant Ponzi scheme. And the accounting system never suggests it might be time to stop.

If we don't stop, all these externalities will continue to increase, damaging society, nature and the environment. Achieving the SDGs will be a distant goal, though I hope some new goals will be set in 2030. Inequality will get worse as if eight men owning the same wealth as the 3.6 billion[2] who make up the poorest half of humanity isn't enough inequality. The period when a middle class was able to gain some control over resources will fade. Those barriers to entry of professional qualifications and selective recruitment that supported lawyers, doctors, estate agents, surveyors, architects, journalists, computing specialists and, how ironic, accountants, are all being eroded by capital, only this time it is capital as information technology and AI.

In a newspaper article, Joseph Stiglitz runs through the implications of widening inequality for an economic system based on unfettered competition saying, 'Some of the increase in market power is the result of changes in technology and economic structure… And some of it reflects the naked abuse and leveraging of market power through the political process.'[3] The United States' 50 wealthiest families held US$1.2 trillion in assets which has grown by just over 1,000 % between 1983 and 2020.[4] This wealth provides political power that can literally shift markets and change the rules by which they operate. Whether this is tech feudalism or neo feudalism or oligarchy, the result is the same. A competitive market economy, with all the benefits that it can provide, is being undermined.

Already there are new calls for reparations for damage done by climate change, and international recognition of the principle that the polluter should pay.[5] In the UK alone, air pollution is killing more than 500 people a week.[6] Globally this was over 8 million people in 2021.[7] The costs of climate change, in developing countries, were estimated to be between US$1 and US$1.8 trillion by 2050.[8] These costs may not be paid and the consequence will be more migration. Additionally, as costs build up, new claims will emerge. The next big one could be claims arising from the damage being done by social media. Litigation has already started – for example, litigation for youth addiction from over 140 school districts in the United States[9] – and is likely to continue as evidence increases of mental health issues[10] and online bullying.[11] On top of all the old externalities, new activities are planned where we do not know the risks, or the potential costs, but are likely to go ahead, for example deep-sea mining.[12] Despite the glimmer of hope from the UN Ocean Conference in June 2025,[13] a moratorium on deep-sea mining is not in the existing High Seas Treaty which was adopted in 2023.

At the same time, technology is changing the world around us faster than we can keep up, either as individuals or as societies. The dark web and bitcoin are only the beginning of marketplaces where transactions will be beyond the purview of national legislation. Robotics and AI will replace jobs, and fast. Research[14] in 2017 by McKinsey calculated that 49% of time spent on work activities could be automated with, 'currently demonstrated technology'. Roll forward to 2023 and after the arrival of AI, this is now 60%.[15] It seems wildly optimistic that any increase in wealth will be mysteriously transferred to those who have been replaced, so they can enjoy a life of comfortable inactivity, despite growing arguments for a minimum income for all. But without this transfer, we would have to believe that there will be an increase in demand for other things that people do, which robots can't, for everyone to still earn something like a living.

Meanwhile, GDP will continue to be used as a measure of success, missing the link between accounting and the increase in 'externalities' or 'the risk of extinction' as it might be better described. Accounting externalizes costs, and it is driving us over the edge. The class that suffers is, as ever, the working class, the class of people that sell their physical labour. Who represents people in these groups in all the discussions about what accounting standards should or shouldn't require? Surely, they should have a voice. The accounting system cannot be defined and managed by accountants or global elites, this is why we are where we are. Accounting is political and people that will experience the worst of all these externalities must be involved.

In case paying for all this harm sounds difficult, it is hardwired into the Universal Declaration of Human Rights, Article 8: 'Everyone has the right to an effective remedy by the competent national tribunals for acts violating the fundamental rights granted him by the constitution or by law.'[16] After all, these costs are often a breach of human rights and competent national tribunals could consider remedy through the accounting system.

We had probably best try to change accounting before it is too late. Although private public and international accounting systems have become more siloed, we can step back and imagine what a more integrated system of standards, regulation and governance would look like and what its purpose would be.

Part 3

What can we do?

The clear solution to businesses being able to make and distribute profits which exclude costs caused by their operations is for business to have to pay those costs. This means changing accounting requirements.[1] Chapter 8 explores the opportunities that exist within the accounting system's existing legal requirements, accounting standards and accounting practice. Chapter 9 sets out a new purpose for accounting and explores the technical implications. Chapter 10 explores how we might gain agreement for change, and plans and timescales for transition and how we can make it happen. After all, as Karl Marx said, 'The philosophers have only interpreted the world, in various ways. The point, however, is to change it.'[2]

Let's not forget what we are transitioning from: an economy where these avoided costs are borne by people on lower incomes and wealth fighting for a living wage; by residents of and immigrants to countries in war and social collapse; an economy where public sector services are struggling to keep up with rising demand; and where nature loss and climate change are bringing us to the edge of our own extinction. Women, people from diverse racial and ethnic backgrounds and the working class have paid the highest cost of wealth inequality, climate change and nature loss, and future generations will risk paying far more.

What follows includes ideas and proposals for reform. However, developing an accounting system without involving the people who will experience the consequences is at the root of the problem. Developing effective solutions will only be possible with them.

Chapter 8

A new purpose and a glimmer of hope

This chapter explores the glimmers of hope, and sometimes rays of sunshine, that lie within existing accounting standards and regulations, and that make it possible to create an accounting system which includes these costs in how profits are calculated.

Accounting is a practical way of providing useful information to make decisions under uncertainty. Both legal requirements and the IFRS Conceptual Framework recognize this uncertainty with some humility. For example, the legal requirement that a company's accounts must give a true and fair view, and the IFRS Conceptual Framework, by stating that the goal of ideal financial reporting is unlikely in the short term. With small changes to the IFRS Conceptual Framework and updated interpretations of existing company legislation, the accounting system can be designed to be consistent with the Golden Rule and give the economic system a new purpose.

This would be the first step – the application of accounting standards so that they require people to do as they would be done to by others, businesses to be held to account for, and compensate those experiencing, any harm caused. The purpose would be an expectation of financial returns subject to doing no harm, recognizing that doing no harm does not mean that no harm will be done, any more than an expectation of financial returns means there will be returns. It means that those experiencing harm will be compensated for their loss of well-being.

Accounting never rests and this would be a stepping stone towards a broader purpose – an expectation of well-being that includes financial returns. Work can continue in parallel to explore an accounting system that accounts for both positive and negative externalities, allocating scarce resources to those activities which create the most positive and least negative changes in well-being. This would seem consistent with the IPSASB's Conceptual Framework and the practice of Cost Benefit Analysis (CBA). It makes sense. But it is probably worth seeing what happens first by aligning accounting with empathy and kindness and with the best of being human.

This change to the purpose would align accounting with other social norms for how we behave, creating a price signal that moves investment away from those businesses that continue to create costs for others. These other norms include:

- the Golden Rule and the basic ethics of most of the world's religions and Indigenous worldviews;
- the UN's Declaration of Human Rights and principle of 'Leave No One Behind'[1] and Guiding Principles for Business and Human Rights;
- the UN's guiding principle of 'Do no harm';[2]
- the OECD's principle that the polluter should pay;
- the objectives, missions and strategy statements of financial and accounting regulators, standards setters and professional bodies that act in the public interest and state that this includes aligning social and private costs and returns;
- the interest and expectations of primary users;
- the interest and expectations of governments through the public sector acting as an agent of citizens, residents and service users;
- the interest and expectations of smaller businesses buying from larger businesses;
- legal expectations of individuals including directors, and to some extent businesses as legal persons, set out under a duty of care; and
- examples of directors taking steps to disclose and recognize these costs.

It would make sense to align accounting with these norms even without all the externalities. Alignment comes with challenges, but it is achievable, and it doesn't close the door on other future developments. This chapter covers private and public accounting and how both address certainty. It then looks at related legislation for directors and companies, before considering the public interest within which both sit. It ends with developments in well-being accounting.

Private sector accounting

Many of the solutions lie in the IFRS Conceptual Framework[3] and it's the first 11 paragraphs that are key. There is some amazing stuff in here. If you are a non-accountant, stick with it. If you are an accountant, you will know all this already, but it is worth a reminder.

Paragraphs 1.2 and 1.3 of the IFRS Conceptual Framework are where the changes to accountability and the development of accounting, considered in Part II of the book, have been formalized. These paragraphs tell us that the objective of financial reporting is to provide information that would be useful to a defined group of users who are making decisions to provide resources to an entity, depending on 'their assessment of both future net cash inflows to the entity and management's stewardship of the entity's economic resources'. The information in financial statements is to be used by a predefined group of people known as primary users. These primary users are existing and potential investors, providers of loan finance and other creditors. And the purpose is an expectation of financial returns. 'The decisions described in paragraph 1.2 depend on the returns that existing and potential investors, lenders and other creditors expect, for example, dividends, principal and interest payments or market price increases.'[4,5] This view of users' expectations is an assumption and sounds so reasonable – after all, who wouldn't want financial returns? It is the source code of our economic system, the reason why our economic decisions and the practical application of fiduciary duty default back to financial returns.

Creating useful information for the primary users means generalizing the expectations behind the decisions. Different expectations mean different decisions and require different information. So, accounting has had to generalize, or standardize, an answer. At the beginning of the year, accountants do not go out to all current (let alone potential) investors and ask them what information they personally would want. Of course not. They use accounting standards. Standards that have assumed that the purpose for the maximum number of users is the expectation of financial returns. The IFRS Conceptual Framework recognizes that this is an assumption and in paragraph 1.8, state that 'The Board, in developing Standards, will seek to provide the information set that will meet the needs of the maximum number of primary users'. Recognizing that the IFRS Conceptual Framework sets out a purpose, in these expectations of primary users, provides hope. It means another purpose is possible.

Accounting standards codify a history where accounting practice was developed by and for rich men as they 'traded' around the world. They made profits (or losses) by internalizing as much income as possible and externalizing as much cost as possible and the accounting system developed to support them. You couldn't make it up. But they did.

As we know, little is known about the expectations and interests of today's asset owners[6] though most 'ownership' is through agents, acting in their interest. Neither is there much information on investor's other characteristics – for example, whether they are male or female – that might help explore different expectations. There is though research to support a possible difference in empathy between males and females.[7] As one of the researchers involved said, 'Females may be more empathic because they really understand your predicaments, your emotional state. They feel it almost under their skin.'[8] We are all on a spectrum from being more selfish to being more empathetic human beings, and at times, influenced by our situation, we will all be more one than the other.[9] But why we would develop standards based on a lack of empathy, at one extreme of this range, is extraordinary.[10]

Human Kind is Rutger Bregman's analysis of the evolutionary advantage of homo sapiens. He argues that the basis of our advantage is kindness, our ability to empathize and act on that understanding of others. Homo sapiens are not particularly fast or strong. We do not have a monopoly on the ability to work together, to combine forces to overcome. Why was it that we survived and Neanderthals became extinct? Kindness. He argues against the commonly held assumption that by nature, human beings are selfish and self-interested, comparing this view with other progressive ideas that mainstream opinion saw as dangerous; the abolition of slavery, the advent of democracy and women's right to vote. Women are also significantly more likely to work in care, nursing and education – sectors where people take care of others and have a direct interest in their well-being, and on which we rely. Sectors where levels of pay are notoriously low.

If the maximum number of primary users, especially investors, are empathetic, then their information needs would only be met if we considered the consequences for, and the dependencies on, other people, which include the financial returns. If an accounting system took costs relating to consequences into account in calculating profits, investment managers would shift resources to businesses with lower negative consequences. This would align the things we invest in with being kind to others, with the Golden Rule and we would close any gap between social and private returns. An accounting system that is built on kindness would, over time, make us all more kind, in the same way as an accounting system built on individual self-interest has made us all more selfish. This is a big glimmer.

There is a long history of social and ethical investing where the social and environmental expectations have been seen as an 'add on'. The financial accounts are based on a calculation of profit that contributes to the various externalities that ethical and social investing seek to address or at least not contribute to.[11] There is a growth in impact investing, where some investors are willing to accept a trade-off between impact and financial goals.[12] Research suggests pension fund members may support investment goals that support social returns, even if there is a trade off with financial performance.[13] In

2024, the FCA's Financial Lives survey reported that 72% of adults who already had investments wanted to 'do some good as well as provide a financial return'.[14] In a survey of American investors in 2025, Moneywise found that 'profit alone isn't enough anymore'.[15] There is increasing evidence of wider expectations of primary users. All glimmers of hope that support a change in purpose.

One way of exploring expectations is to ask people. Social Value International (SVI) tested this in an online survey in 2024, and I regularly use this approach. I start with a simple multiple-choice question, 'Do you want financial returns from your investments? Yes or No.' Not surprisingly this gets a 100% 'Yes'. But this is just the set up. The next question comes with some options:

'What sort of returns do you expect from your investments?'

1. Financial returns and no interest in any other social or environmental consequences.
2. Financial returns and no negative social or environmental consequences (doing no harm).
3. Financial returns and net positive social or environmental consequences.
4. Social and environmental returns and a minimum financial return.
5. Social and environmental returns and no interest in financial returns.

The first option is what everyone who said 'Yes' to the first question voted for. When it becomes obvious that this isn't a holistic question, nearly everyone shifts to either option 2 or option 3, including accounting students and accounting professors. In SVI's survey with very similar questions, 3% of people chose option 1 (only financial returns), but 1% chose option 5 (only social and environmental returns). The majority chose options 2 and 3. SVI expect to test this in a larger international survey.

If you are still not convinced, try another quote from Adam Smith. 'How selfish soever man may be supposed, there are evidently some principles in his nature, which interest him in the fortune of others, and render their happiness necessary to him, though he derives nothing from it except the pleasure of seeing it.'[16]

IAS 37 'Provisions, Contingent Liabilities and Contingent Assets', already allows for directors to internalize externalities. Paragraph 4.32 of the IFRS Conceptual Framework refers to constructive obligations, that 'can also arise, however, from an entity's customary practices, published policies or specific statements if the entity has no practical ability to act in a manner inconsistent with those practices, policies or statements'. This is applicable even when the recipient has not been identified (para 4.29). An obligation, whether legal or constructed, means that the business has no realistic way of avoiding making a payment, they have become 'liabilities' in accounting language. Or, in plainer terms, they have become 'costs' – part of that production cost. A constructive obligation was defined in Chapter 2. If the requirements of a constructive obligation are met, this allows directors to accept responsibility for costs that have been imposed on others as a consequence of the business's operations. Cost can be constructed without a contract, though a constructive obligation could become a contract with the relevant third party. Given the dependence on contracts to determine cost everywhere else, this is nothing short of amazing, more of a ray of sunshine than a glimmer of hope. And it is worth remembering that recognizing the cost creates an immediate incentive to make changes to reduce both impacts and dependencies.

If users have other expectations, we wouldn't call it 'financial' accounting, we would call it 'financial and other expectations' accounting. Even if we accept that investors do need other information, there might be an argument that this is what non-financial reporting (including Environmental, Social and Governance (ESG)) is already providing and is increasingly a legal requirement, at least for larger businesses. In which case financial accounting can just stick to being financial accounting. This argument is a good try, perhaps even a cunning try, but it misses the point. If investors have different expectations, then the accounts should reflect them. The information should be provided in one place, with one logic and one account. If our expectation is financial returns, that is profits, recognizing costs of harm done, those costs should be part of how profits are calculated.

Public sector accounting

Just in case there's any doubt, the public sector still represents a significant share of the world economy and is a major investor in public infrastructure and services. Government raises finance through tax and through bond issues. In 2022 the global bond market was US$133 trillion[17] and sovereign bonds, or public debt, accounted for over 60% of the global bond market.[18]

There is another Conceptual Framework designed for organizations that are owned by the public; the Conceptual Framework for General Purpose Financial Reporting by Public Sector Entities.[19] Snappy, but it does what it says on the tin. Chapter 2 is a thing of beauty. It has nailed the question of the user, their decisions and the purpose behind their decisions. It states that:

- the objectives of financial reporting by public sector entities, 'are to provide information that is useful to users of General Purpose Financial Reports (GPFRs) for accounting purposes and for decision making purposes';[20]
- the purpose of those decisions relates to the primary purpose of government which is, 'to provide services that enhance or maintain the well-being of citizens and other eligible residents';
- primary users of GPFRs are, 'service recipients and resource providers and their representatives' where resource providers include taxpayers, lenders and donors; and the type of information to discharge those accountability obligations, 'will also require the provision of information about such matters as the entities' service delivery achievements during the reporting period'.[21]

Well-being is already at the heart of public sector accounting standards. The public has two interests: first, 'How was my money spent?' and second, 'What happened to my well-being as a result?' Separating the answer to these questions has led to a difference between public sector accounting (how my money was spent) and CBA (what is expected to happen because of that expenditure).

This goes even further than negative externalities. It would imply that the scope would be positive and negative changes to well-being, recognizing trade-offs and distributional effects, as in CBA. We've already argued that governments are interested in more than only financial returns when they raise taxes. There is no point raising money only to spend it addressing any 'externalities' caused by businesses paying tax. CBA has been used to guide public expenditure for many years. In the UK, this is set out in the Green Book[22,23] which includes an appendix on well-being. Most governments use some form of CBA to look at non-financial benefits to inform expenditure and investment decisions and have been using approaches to valuing these non-financial benefits for many years.

You might also assume that once the money is spent, public sector approaches to accounting would allow users to see how well reality matched plans. Well, it could. All we need to do is account for actual changes in well-being – and be able to compare the two! There is a non-authoritative practice guideline that relates to service performance which would be a basis from which to start, *Recommended Practice Guidance (RPG) 3, Reporting Service Performance Information*,[24,25] and there are amendments relating to reporting on sustainability programmes.[26] And New Zealand's External Reporting Board, XRB, has recently released a voluntary conceptual framework for consider how to articulate long term intergenerational impact on people and planet.[27]

This is another glimmer of hope. It would be possible to develop public accounting standards to account for well-being and so that provision of information on performance in relation to enhancing and maintaining well-being would be, well, standard. Not that every member of the public will be spending Sunday afternoons poring over the accounts any more than you might look at the accounts of any of the companies in your pension pot. But the way in which they are prepared should be based on providing information to those with the interest set out in the IPSASB Conceptual Framework.

Accounting and levels of certainty

In Paragraph 1.11, the IFRS Conceptual Framework recognizes that, 'To a large extent, financial reports are based on estimates, judgements and models rather than exact depictions.' Realizing that a level of certainty is required for information to be useful opens the possibility of changing that level of certainty. A generalized user with an additional expectation that no harm is done (and any harm is being compensated) may not need the same level of certainty for that information to be useful. They may be happy with less certain information being included, so that there is a lower risk they make decisions that result in those negative consequences.

The IFRS Conceptual Framework defines 'expenditure' as 'decreases in assets, or increases in liabilities, that result in decreases in equity, other than those relating to distributions to holders of equity claims'.[28] Paragraph 4.37 allows for a potential transfer of an economic resource (e.g. money) 'even if it is not certain, or even likely, that the entity will be required to transfer an economic resource'. How uncertain? Make this level a bit less certain and more liabilities would be recognized. Another glimmer of hope?

You can probably hear the cries of 'but that won't be fair' already. But ignoring these costs, imposes costs on others. Hardly fair. This is why we need that change in purpose, which will also change the level of certainty required, to at least reflect the requirement for primary users to act in the interests of those affected.

Company legislation and directors' duties

Duty to produce accounts

It is the directors' responsibility to produce financial accounts. Delegation doesn't remove that responsibility. In many countries, the responsibility is to produce accounts that provide a true and fair view of the financial position and performance of a company. The words change a bit, the scope changes a bit, but the essence is the same.

Remember the East India Company? Preparing accounts 'truely and fairely'. And cast your mind back to the just and fair weighing of good and bad deeds on Judgement Day. Generally, the legislation refers to the standards that directors use to provide information on the financial position and performance of the business. The legislation makes it easier by telling them which accounting standards to use.

But directors must be careful not to abdicate their responsibilities to the professionals. The relevant legislation in the UK is the Companies Act 2006 in s393 to s396. Section 393 states that 'the directors of a company must not approve accounts… unless they are satisfied that they give a true and fair view of the assets, liabilities, financial position and profit or loss'. Section 395 addresses the applicable accounting framework, permitting UK adopted international accounting standards or as required in s396. And s396 is the one that makes it clear that directors, not accountants, are responsible and includes the clause:

> (5) If in special circumstances compliance with any of those provisions is inconsistent with the requirement to give a true and fair view, the directors must depart from that provision to the extent necessary to give a true and fair view. Particulars of any such departure, the reasons for it and its effect must be given in a note to the accounts.

If it is necessary to add information or to depart from a provision to give a true and fair view, directors *must* do so.

This is also a requirement in many other jurisdictions, including, for example, the European Union,[29] Spain,[30,31,32] India,[33] Malaysia,[34] Australia[35] and Indonesia.[36] There are many more examples, and while each jurisdiction will have different interpretations of what this means in practice, there do appear to be a couple of consistent principles:

- It's a legal duty for directors to approve accounts that give a true and fair view.
- The duty trumps accounting standards. In other words, directors must add information that is not required to

> conform with financial reporting standards used in their jurisdiction if necessary to give a true and fair view.

In the UK, what it means to be true and fair is not legally defined, and the FRC provide guidance[37] based on a barrister's opinion, last updated on FRC's website in 2014. The guidance states:

> True and fair is not something that is merely a separate add on to accounting standards. Rather the whole essence of standards is to provide for recognition, measurement, presentation and disclosure for specific aspects of financial reporting in a way that reflects economic reality and hence that provides a true and fair view.

Powerful stuff.

The FRC's report highlights the importance of professional judgement and provides examples of where this is required including, among others:

> Not using detailed accounting rules as an excuse for poor accounting.
>
> Considering what is and what is not material.
>
> Giving appropriate disclosures even where not specifically required by accounting standards.
>
> Standing back at the end of the accounts process and making sure the accounts overall do give a true and fair view.[38]

The problem is that the world has changed since 2014 and all those 'sustainability issues' are now at a critical point to both our global society and to business. Some of those issues are external but some are the result of the existing business model. Understanding the potential risks to the business arising from the existing business model over the last reporting period is critical to an understanding of the true and fair position of a company.

This is not just a legal nicety. The dominant company structure today is the limited liability company. It has been the bedrock for extraordinary growth in investment and in the value created for customers over the last 200 years. It reflects a social contract. You can have limited liability as owners of a company and in return you must provide information that gives a true and fair reflection of the value you have created. The harm being caused to people and the environment because of the way in which true and fair is interpreted is undermining the competitiveness and resilience of businesses to these risks, and the social contract.

There are directors that are recognizing these challenges. One example is Kering, the holding company for major international brands including Brioni, Bottega Veneta and Gucci among others. Kering produces an annual environmental profit and loss account which calculates the group's negative effect on the environment, and values it. For 2023, this was €498m,[39] 15% of free cash flow (excluding real estate acquisition) of €3,321m.[40] In other words, the directors recognize that the profit they made for shareholders, and the value gained by their customers and employees, came at a cost to the environment that will have negative impacts on people's lives. It is great to see this level of transparency. Imagine if Kering accepted responsibility for these costs and made a commitment to pay those costs that a third party expected would be met, a constructive obligation. This amount would become a liability and a cost in the financial profit and loss account, necessary for the accounts to be true and fair; and social and environmental costs would have become economic costs

This is more than just a glimmer of hope. There is a light shining through the gap between international accounting standards and the requirement for accounts to give a true and fair view. There are examples of smaller companies where the directors have decided that information about their use of carbon in the year relating to the accounts must be added to give a true and fair view, information that does not relate to any items disclosed in the balance sheet or the profit and loss account.

Note 25 from the audited accounts of Felix Midco Ltd,[41] the parent company of TrustedHousesitters, for the period ended 31 December 2024[42] states,

> Under UK company law, directors must not approve the financial statements unless they are satisfied that they give a

> true and fair view and to that end, Felix Midco Ltd wishes to clarify that the calculated profit for the period does not include the cost of our continued contribution to climate change via our use of carbon.
>
> Felix Midco's estimated carbon emissions across Scope 1, 2 and 3 are calculated by Greenly using a mix of accountancy-based and activity-based data and the evaluation of our emissions follows the standards of the GHG protocol methodology. Felix Midco generated 792 tco_2e. Using the Government's Valuation of Greenhouse Gas Emissions for Policy Appraisal and Evaluation quoted cost of carbon for 2024 of £256 per tonne, Felix Midco's financial impact of carbon use is £201k on this basis. The amount is not accounted for in these financial statements in any way.

SVI commissioned a legal opinion on the true and fair requirement from a leading KC, George Bompas[43] to explore the requirement in the context of sustainability. There is a lot in the 27 pages of the opinion, but a couple of things stand out. Alongside reminding readers of relevant sections of the Companies Act 2006, including that any necessary additional information to give a true and fair view might be in the accounts or in the notes to the accounts, his opinion in relation to sustainability related information concluded, in paragraph 43:

> In summary, therefore, directors and auditors, considering whether the True and Fair Requirement has been met by them as regards any particular annual accounts, must be aware of possible impacts on the financial report flowing from sustainability-related issues,[44] just as they must in the case of any other areas of material risk or probable or possible change which may be relevant to their company's activities.'

The legal opinion included a discussion on possible types of disclosure and included the possibility that directors may actively want to make concrete sustainability commitments that create constructive obligations. This is nothing short of amazing. It blows apart the idea that externalities are some sort of inevitable and unavoidable consequence of a market economy to be fixed by government. Stop and make a cup of tea and take a moment to reflect.

It turns out that many of those externalities are the result of a choice. Directors could choose to structure commitments that include these costs by creating constructive obligations. SVI produced guidance in 2025, 'Are your accounts True and Fair?', for both UK[45] and Spanish[46] directors, providing examples under common law and civil law. The guidance includes an example, 'The directors, recognizing the systemic risks to the business from climate change and the costs to society, accept responsibility to pay for the consequences of their carbon use for the current year.' SVI put this into practice in their 2023/24 accounts where the Trustees report recognized the use of carbon as a cost of doing business.[47] Accounting standards are way ahead! Directors can accept responsibility for those costs and internalize them or decide that the information is required as a note for the accounts to give a true and fair view. The language may be rarified, but that is why it is beautiful.

Directors often have little time to consider the true and fair requirement. In a blog[48] in 2023, referring to the requirement in India, Bharat Vasani and Varun Kannan from Cyril Amarchand Mangaldas, an Indian law firm, went as far as to suggest that, 'Given the mad rush with which this process is completed, and the exclusive reliance on confirmations/representations provided by somebody else, nobody can put their hand on heart and confirm how true the "true and fair view" is.'

Climate change is one risk but there are others, contribution to water use and pollution, soil degradation, reduction of habitat, dependency on low or unpaid wages to name a few. The Task Force on Climate-related Financial Disclosures (TCFD)'s risk taxonomy covers policy and legal, technology, market and reputation and many companies are now disclosing information against the Task Force on Nature-related Financial Disclosures (TNFD)[49] and the TCFD.[50] Directors have a responsibility to consider whether the business model is contributing to any of these risks and consider whether additional information (to what is required by relevant accounting standards) should be added to the accounts for that true and fair view, even if it has been disclosed elsewhere, strengthening the links between risk analysis, the risk register and financial reporting.

Duty to promote the success of the company

Directors have many other legal duties that come up in many countries' company legislation. In the UK. one responsibility is the duty to promote the success of the company set out in s172 of the Companies Act 2006:

> (1) A director of a company must act in the way he considers, in good faith, would be most likely to promote the success of the company for the benefit of its members as a whole, and in doing so have regard (among other matters) to –
> (a) the likely consequences of any decision in the long term,
> (b) the interests of the company's employees,
> (c) the need to foster the company's business relationships with suppliers, customers and others,
> (d) the impact of the company's operations on the community and the environment,
> (e) the desirability of the company maintaining a reputation for high standards of business conduct, and
> (f) the need to act fairly as between members of the company.
>
> (2) Where or to the extent that the purposes of the company consist of or include purposes other than the benefit of its members, subsection (1) has effect as if the reference to promoting the success of the company for the benefit of its members were to be achieving those purposes.

All of which recognizes the need to take the effect of decisions on other stakeholders into account. Clause (2) suggests that if you have a different purpose to benefiting members, interpreted as financial returns, then directors must act to promote that different purpose. This raises the question of how they will do that if they do not develop an accounting system that is fit for that other purpose? There is more than a glimmer in all this.

Redefining the purpose of a business, for example being a responsible business, taking responsibility for costs imposed on others, would have bigger implications for what is true and fair. Charities are another example. Their purpose is improving the lives of their beneficiaries and charities prepare accounts based on a Statement of Recommended Practice (SORP) as a supplement to FRS 102. Though perhaps it should say more about the extent to which the charity has improved or not beneficiaries' lives, if the accounts are to give a true and fair view?

What exactly does it mean to promote the success of the company? Climate change may be a great example of the free rider problem because unless we all do our part, any sort of success becomes unlikely. Arguing for and supporting national and global carbon reduction initiatives will be promoting the long-term success of a company. Showing the way forward by including this information in the accounts will be promoting the success of the company. Recognizing that business will have to deal with increasing costs arising from climate change, and potential increases in direct costs from their own use of carbon, will encourage decisions to reduce those costs and promote the success of the company.

Directors' duty to promote the success of the company (also termed 'duty of loyalty') is common in many jurisdictions.[51] The United States has Benefit Corporations which require consideration of social and environmental goals, and the German Corporate Governance Code requires consideration of employees and other stakeholders.[52] In France the PACTE Law 2019 introduced the concept of a company's 'raison d'être' (purpose) into corporate law and companies may now register as 'société à mission', requiring them to pursue social and environmental missions alongside profit.[53] In 2017, the British Academy started a project on the Future of the Corporation,[54] the ISO is developing a standard on Purpose Driven Organisations, and the Standing International Forum of Commercial Courts discussed purpose during its 2024 meeting in Doha.[55]

All more glimmers.

Directors' duty of care

Section 174 (1) of the UK Companies Act 2006 states that 'A director of a company must exercise reasonable care, skill and diligence', a duty under company law that is common in other jurisdictions. A new recent UK legal opinion[56] on nature related risks and directors' duties suggested that directors should consider climate and biodiversity impacts and dependencies in order to understand whether they create risks and opportunities to the company – otherwise they could be breaching these duties.[57]

Companies' duty of care

Outside of company law, there are general civil law duties between people, including companies. This is governed in England by Tort Law – which addresses wrongful behaviour that causes harm or loss to another person or their property (including negligence). While the idea of rights may currently be under attack, or at least becoming harder to enforce, duties are the flip side of rights. A duty not to steal implies a right not be to stolen from. A duty of care implies a right to be cared for. The question might be who has this right? You might hope this includes people on whom costs have been imposed that they have not agreed to and probably not been paid to accept. If the company owes a duty of care and has breached it, and the breach caused foreseeable harm, then perhaps. Directors might consider some of what comes under the heading of sustainability issues or impact, at least for any negative impacts, from the perspective of their decisions to meet a company's duty of care. There is a lot of case law on this. At its heart is the concept of reasonable care, tested against the standard of a reasonable person.[58] A reasonable person will consider probable losses to others, make plans to avoid causing harm to others and take as much care of others as they would of themselves. Yes, it is the Golden Rule again. For a company, the duty of reasonable care can relate to stakeholders, those whose well-being might be affected by an organization.

In 1990, in *Caparo Industries plc v Dickman*, a three-stage test for duty of care was established: Was it foreseeable? Was there a close relationship between the parties? Is it fair to impose a duty?

But a company's duty of care may be harder to enforce. Despite being a person in law, it is the directors and employees who execute a company's actions. In most negligence cases against a company, the claimant must show that the company, through its employees or management, failed to take reasonable care and caused harm to a legal person. Some jurisdictions have recognized the rights of nature in law,[59] for example Ecuador recognized the rights of nature in its constitution in 2008 and, in *Huddle v. Provincial Government of Loja*, the court ruled in favour of nature, with the Provincial Government of Loja required to present a remediation and rehabilitation plan of the Vilcabamba River. This is getting close to nature sending in an invoice.

Relevant legislation has been tightening. In 2007, the UK's Corporate Manslaughter and Corporate Homicide Act made it possible to hold an organization, as a legal person, criminally liable in cases of serious failings in management amount to a gross breach of duty of care. In 2021, in a case brought by four Nigerian Farmers and Friends of the Earth, a Dutch Appeals court held that Royal Dutch Shell's Nigerian subsidiary was responsible for multiple oil pipeline leaks and should pay unspecified damages to affected farmers. In New Zealand, Michael John Smith, a Māori elder, brought a case against seven corporate defendants alleging that their greenhouse gas emissions contributed significantly to climate change, thereby harming his customary lands and cultural heritage. The case *Smith v Fonterra Co-operative* went all the way to Australia's Supreme Court, which concluded in 2024 that there was at least a case to answer. In 2025, a Peruvian farmer's lawsuit against German utility RWE, claiming his home had been put at risk by the company's emissions, was dismissed because the estimated 1% risk of flooding over 30 years was not considered sufficiently serious or imminent. Crucially, however, the case set a precedent for using climate science to show liability for damage caused by greenhouse gas emissions. The German court acknowledged that major emitters could be held liable if causation and risk thresholds were met.[60] According to the Grantham Institute report on global trends in climate change litigation, at least 226 climate cases were filed in 2024.[61] Legal recognition of liabilities increases the risk that businesses will be held accountable for these costs. There might be another glimmer or two here.

Audit

Auditing standards are good and can be turned to auditing information relating to our new purpose. 'ISA 540 Auditing Accounting Estimates and related disclosures'[62] already reinforces the point that accounts include estimates and this is fine, and they can be audited. 'ISA 315, Identifying and Assessing the Risks of Material Misstatement'[63] recognizes that there will always be a risk that some information is missing or added – information that matters to or influences a decision. There may be a need to update skills to be able to audit information relating to constructive obligations to pay for that harm. But the basic proposition and the basic principles are fine.

Public interest

It is time to cycle back to the role of accountancy and audit in the context of the public interest, where directors must approve accounts that give a true and fair view, and auditors must also provide an opinion of whether the accounts provide that true and fair view.

As it stands, how is it possible to conclude that accounts which exclude externalities give a true and fair view and align with a public interest that would include aligning social and private returns? If these costs are excluded, it should surely be an issue for regulators, or time to update some of those public interest statements. A reinterpretation of the true and fair requirement within the context of the public interest would then ensure that alignment. If the audit opinion was required to address completeness of both legal and constructed obligations (to avoid externalities) it would be closer to the public interest. Another possible ray of sunshine. An argument in favour of efficient resource allocation in markets and the public interest may also be a strong argument in favour of reconsidering the purpose behind private sector financial accounting.

If it is not in the public interest to have a difference between social and private returns, then a voluntary approach to constructing obligations which internalize externalities is not enough to meet the public interest. Though you can see why it meets the interests of the shareholders (remembering that these are increasingly investment manager agents acting on behalf of their principals). Yes, this may have implications for businesses in the short term, but the basis of a market economy is competition. Cost is a driver of innovation and new businesses will start that are less dependent on the excluded costs. Oligopolies are bad because they suppress competition and do not respond to customers at the rate they would have to if there were competition. Creative destruction, businesses starting and closing, is a form of assurance that reduces risk.

The existing public interest statements could probably do with a refresh, and better if written by those who tell the organizations what their public interest is. They could perhaps add clarity on where they come from, how and when they are updated and how exactly people hold them to account and for what. The IFRS Foundation public interest statement is a good example. It includes the reference to accountability which sounds like a good thing. The ability of '*the* providers of capital to hold the people to whom they have entrusted their money to *account*'. The IFRS Conceptual Framework says that the primary users need information to allow them to assess the economic position of a business and how efficiently and effectively management[64] have discharged their responsibilities.[65] The reference in the public interest statement might change to say 'the providers of *capital and those experiencing the consequences of that provision*, to hold the people to whom they have entrusted their money *to account for those consequences, which include the financial returns*, and how efficiently management have discharged their responsibilities.'

A bias towards current generations, built on an assumption that the future will find a solution, is quite common and masks a conflict between the interests of different sections of the public. The IFAC's statement had that reference to public interest in net benefits 'in relation to any action, decision or policy'.[66] Resolving this conflict would require IFAC to provide members with guidance on how to account for the trade-offs between both benefits and costs and between different sections of the public including future generations. Existing accounting standards don't account for these trade-offs. If that seems a tough request, it may be worth remembering that this is an existing requirement of the UK Government, in the context of the requirements for Charities[67] includes, 'any detriment or harm that results from the purpose (to people, property or the environment) must not outweigh the benefit – this is also based on evidence and not on personal views'. The statement also raises a different issue. In the section of IFAC's statement describing 'The interests of the public', there is reference to public interest in 'the minimisation of natural resource depletion'. Very good though perhaps would need to become something like 'sustaining eco-systems'.

It is hard enough to recognize the scale of the problem, remembering accountancy's reputation for being so dull. It is even harder to recognize that accounting is a public good and that all this is a question of public policy, of what the legislation says in each country's company legislation, and how this is interpreted and applied in practice. But it is starting to happen and Thomas Aquinas's just price has reemerged in France. In a report in response to concerns over private equity investments in the medical laboratory sector the regulators, L'Igas/IGF, said that 'measures must be taken to bring the cost of biology back to a 'juste prix'.[68]

Public interest is national but informed by international agreements. Every few years the UN holds a Finance for Development conference. The first was in 2002 in Mexico and the most recent in Sevilla in 2025, where the heads of state adopted the 'Compromiso de Sevilla' and committed to continued reform of the international financial architecture, 'enhancing its resilience, coherence and effectiveness in responding to present and future challenges and crises. To better reflect today's realities, we commit to make global economic governance more inclusive, representative, equitable and effective.' More specifically it included a reference to 'internalising externalities'.[69] Public policy is catching up.

Work on well-being accounting

We have already seen that well-being is becoming more integrated in international and national governments' approaches to assessing performance and the health of an economy. And that the IPSASB already refers to well-being. Glimmers of hope for a well-being economy. In the overview of their book *Beyond Profit: Purpose-Driven Leadership for a Well-being Economy*[70] Ben Renshaw, Victoria Hurth and Lorenzo Fioramonti say:

> We have reached a critical moment where we must confront the central issue driving our unsustainable world: the profit motive. In other words, we have created governance systems to ensure our decisions maximize financial self-interest – in the assumption this will achieve collective long-term well-being (sustainability). However, putting profit, and ourselves, at the centre of the room is both the root cause of our unsustainability and also what has held us back from solving the resulting crises. It makes harm to our sustained collective well-being a logical outcome. A profit-first world isn't just stifling innovation; it's accelerating the decline of well-being for all life on earth.

The ISO is working on a standard for Purpose Driven Organizations, ISO 37011, that puts well-being at the heart of purpose.[71] The UNDP SDG Impact Standards use well-being as a unit of account for positive and negative consequences of decisions, to maximize the contribution to sustainable development and the SDGs.[72] A case study, Seed and Co, based on these standards, shows what this approach would like in practice.[73] These, and other work on integrated profit and loss accounts (more in the next chapter), are starting to explore management's stewardship in relation to externalities and well-being.

This is all a good start, but to change from accounting for financial returns to accounting for well-being is more challenging. At some point, well-being accounting would need to account for positive and negative externalities at the level of transactions. There is much to learn from financial accounting.

Chapter 9

Changing accounting and auditing

This chapter is probably more for accountants. There are challenges to defining and then providing useful information that can seem insurmountable. Accounting and auditing standards, as part of the accounting system, are a brilliant solution to these challenges.

The first part of this chapter compares the existing approach with the changes necessary to be able to account for harm done, as the basis of compensating for that harm and recognizing the cost in the accounts. The second part explores some, but only some, of the issues that would need to be addressed if profit was calculated taking both positive and negative changes to well-being into account.

Accounting for negative externalities (or loss in well-being or harm done)

The change is to the basis on which we create useful information, a change that will change behaviours and the innovations that entrepreneurs bring to the market. Table 9.1 is a summary, based on the structure of useful information set out in the IFRS Conceptual Framework, followed by further detail. Not much needs to change which makes things easier.

Table 9.1: Changes to requirements for useful information

Comparison of approaches	**Current**	**New**
Purpose	Financial returns	Financial returns subject to do no harm
Primary users	Current and potential investors, providers of loan finance and other creditors	Add clarity that this refers to investors as the principals, the beneficial owners Add government with the government acting in both the interest of primary users and those experiencing negative consequences
Information needed for those decisions	Economic resources controlled by the entity (assets) and claims against those resources (liabilities) Management's stewardship of those resources	Remains the same, although liabilities now include previously externalized costs
Relevant	Information that can make a difference to decisions made by primary users	Remains the same
Faithfully represented	Complete, neutral and free from error	Remains the same
Elements	Assets, liabilities, income, expenditure, equity	Remain the same although there is an option for equity

Table 9.1: Continued

Comparison of approaches	Current	New
Recognition and disclosure	Existing, outcome and measurement uncertainty	Same issues but may require change to level of uncertainty for disclosure/recognition and more information in notes
Measurement	Monetary terms	Remains the same but with the payment for externalities valued by reference to well-being
Concepts of capital and capital maintenance	Financial capital is the net assets or equity of the entity Physical capital is a business's productive capacity	Remains the same
Public interest	Varied but often refers to efficient markets	Includes alignment of private and social costs and returns, specifically avoidance of negative externalities

Purpose

To start with, we just need to add a couple of words to paragraph 1.3 in the IFRS Conceptual Framework and update the purpose. Paragraph 1.3 should become something like: 'The decisions described in paragraph 1.2 depend on the financial returns *and the absence of harm to others* that existing and potential investors, lenders and other creditors expect.'

Primary users

In the 2001 version of the IFRS Conceptual Framework, adopted from the IASC, government was included in the list of primary users. We need to add it back in. Government, acting in the interests of residents, citizens and services users (which will include investors, providers of loan finance or other creditors) is the biggest user of accounts. And government is not only interested in financial returns when acting in those interests. In the UK, FRS102 also include employees and members of the public as users which also raises the question of whether their expectations are the same as other users. With the change in purpose above, the decision is still whether to provide resources to the entity but for government, as a user, it now includes whether to provide resources to address any harm done by an entity.

Relevant

Information is relevant if it is capable of making a difference in the decisions made by primary users, but what then makes information material? Paragraph 2.11 from the Conceptual Framework says:

> Information is material if omitting, misstating or obscuring it could reasonably be expected to influence decisions that the primary users of general-purpose financial reports (see paragraph 1.5) make on the basis of those reports, which provide financial information about a specific reporting entity. In other words, materiality is an entity-specific aspect of relevance based on the nature or magnitude, or both, of the items to which the information relates in the context of an individual entity's financial report. Consequently, the Board cannot specify a uniform quantitative threshold for materiality or predetermine what could be material in a particular situation.[1]

This, then, is information that would matter if it was missed out by mistake or through fraud, or has been misstated, or included and obscures other useful information. It might not be recognized or disclosed because of issues around certainty but it is 'in'. Just think about accounting for buying a pencil. Accountants don't get to go, 'Oh but it is too small so we can leave it out'; it is relevant and it is accounted for. Though auditors are unlikely to worry if one had been missed out; it is not material. It is accounted for as many smalls add up to one big. And if you are forecasting that it will be small, it might turn out not to be. If there is harm done to anyone, and they incur costs, whether financial or otherwise, following from a business' operations, this would be relevant.

Faithfully represented

This means complete, neutral and free from error (or sufficiently so to meet the level of certainty we require for useful information). Nothing to change here. Critically, the information that goes into the financial statements does not need to be comparable. Comparability enhances the value of information, but it is not a requirement! This may seem surprising, but comparability of financial statements arises from consistent application of accounting standards supported by audit, not from consistency of the inputs. Compare this with the enthusiasm for standardizing sustainability metrics as an input to a sustainability report.

Whether negative changes in well-being can be faithfully represented hinges on a required level of certainty, which would need to be reassessed. This will allow some generalized rules to be developed, so that the risk that any negative changes are missing, that would have affected a decision, is brought down to a level that is acceptable. Many of these consequences will flow from the existing transactions. Not all perhaps, but most can be linked back to a transaction. Both measurement and assessment of causation will need to be estimated, based on models, just like it says in the IFRS Conceptual Framework. Initial estimates could be based on industry wide averages, or expenditure type averages. This is happening already in carbon accounting (explored, for example, by Accounting Streams[2]) through software that is available an add-on to existing financial accounting packages. An approach that can be mirrored for other consequences. Accounting for inequality could be informed by the Organisation for Economic Co-operation and Development's (OECD) guidance on measuring and valuing income inequality[3] which may need some software and an app to make it more accessible. Unemployed labour in supply chains might be harder, but an estimate is still possible.

Elements

Including the costs relating to a business's contribution to externalities doesn't need a new element. The elements remain assets, liabilities, income, expenditure and equity. There is, though, an option for how equity is treated. So far, the obligation for transfer of an economic resource for any contribution to externalities has been met by a payment. Another option might be to issue equity, or shares, to that value to a legal person acting in the interest of those experiencing the externality, if this met the requirement for a transfer of an economic resource. This could be someone acting on behalf of unpaid labour, or on behalf of nature, where legislation has given nature the rights of a legal person, holding the shares in trust. This may seem more appropriate as it is the interest of the investors who have been benefiting from returns that didn't take these costs into account that is being diluted. Well, it's an idea, building on other thinking about corporate governance for nature.[4]

The elements are one of the big challenges for accounting for positive and negative impacts, as accounting for positive impacts that are not owned by the company. This would raise a bigger conceptual issue, considered below.

Recognition and disclosure

If the information is relevant to a user's decision, a decision to provide resources to an entity, based on the resources of that entity and management's stewardship of those resources (a reflection of management's decisions), and can be faithfully represented, the information should be in the accounts. Perhaps the best place for disclosure is in the notes, but the information should still be there.

Inevitably a line must be drawn somewhere. Information on one side of the line becomes disclosed if it meets these requirements. Information on the other side of the line does not. But where the line is drawn arises from historical practice. If we need to move it for the information to be complete, we can change what is required for faithful representation. The key is that information must be useful to users making decisions with a new purpose.

This also overlaps with a transition from these costs being excluded to being included. Initially the information could be required as a note, disclosed, but not recognized, in the balance sheet and the profit and loss account. But if the users are to get the information required in paragraph 1.4 of the IFRS Conceptual Framework, on, 'how efficiently and effectively the entity's management and governing board have discharged their responsibilities to use the entity's economic resources', the harm will need to shift over time to be recognized in the balance sheet and profit and loss account, as well as in the notes.

Measurement

In accounting, measurement means represented in monetary units. Of course it does. But not only because accounting is about money. If you are going to compare different things and make decisions choosing between different ways of achieving your purpose, you will need a common unit.

For some people, representing changes in people's well-being in monetary units is difficult and why courts may have tended to assess damages in relation to economic losses. The reality is, in making investment decisions between different opportunities, the consequences and potential harm would be different, and experienced by different people, so a common unit is necessary for trade-offs to be transparent. Done well it would also ensure that, for example, negative impacts above thresholds set by planetary boundaries and social norms would have very high relative values. We already use proxies for estimating the change in well-being, for example, carbon emissions. We can then estimate the amount that would be necessary to compensate for the negative change in well-being. This is the social cost of carbon. Estimation is not a barrier to recognition or disclosure and this can all be handled within existing accounting standards as a constructive obligation.

The idea of a 'fair' value comes from IFRS 13 Fair Value[5] where fair value is 'the price that would be received to sell an asset or paid to transfer a liability in an orderly transaction between market participants at the measurement date'. 'Orderly' means not forced or distressed, between willing market participants. They may be willing, but if the valuation is based on excluding costs arising from the transaction, is it really a fair value? Fair value for a constructive obligation cannot be based on this definition as there is no market. The value is fair not because of a market transaction but in the relationship between the principle, do no harm, the specific commitment and whether the amount being paid is a fair estimate. There is a lot of practice now on what this would be, rooted in cost benefit analysis. Impact valuation in the not-for-profit and private sector has been increasing, building on work by many organizations using monetization and other quantitative techniques to value changes in well-being of both people and planet. SVI supports the Impact Valuation Hub[6] and the Capitals Coalition has supported the Value Accounting Network[7] and the Value Commission[8] all of which encourage transparency and improve practice. Businesses like GIST Impact,[9] Simetrica-Jacobs,[10] Valuing Impact[11] and ESVD[12] have developed approaches to well-being valuation that have grown out of CBA. And businesses like House of Hackney, Kering, Olam and Natura are exploring integrated profit and loss accounts. The Capitals Coalition has released a report on 'Emerging Approaches of Integrated Profit and Loss and Impact statements'.[13]

Nonetheless, the strength of markets is that they reflect what people are willing to pay, and a constructive obligation should reflect what people expect to be paid in compensation for harm done. A process that relies only on expert valuation, not rooted in research on what those experiencing harm expect, would be a risky departure for a proxy value that should mirror a process where customers determine price. At the same time a low valuation, and a low cost, might mean no change to decisions which would miss the point. A high valuation and a high cost – and prices might rise more quickly than entrepreneurs can respond to, with too many businesses failing too quickly. The challenge for transition is that valuation of externalities also needs to be commensurate with a rate of decisions – a rate that allows for a change in business models, closure of some and opening of others, fast enough to avoid social and economic crises, but not so fast that it adds to those crises.

Where does the payment go?

The requirement is that there has been an outflow of an economic resource. You cannot get something in return for this payment, as then you will no longer be meeting the original obligation. But who gets paid? IAS 37, paragraph 20 starts, 'An obligation always involves another party to whom the obligation is owed. It is not necessary, however, to know the identity of the party to whom the obligation is owed—indeed the obligation may be to the public at large.' Which is perhaps not very helpful. SVI's guidance, relating to directors choosing to construct obligations, says the payment should be to an organization that is addressing the directors' commitment for which they constructed the obligation. If you are paying for your use of carbon, there is not much point then making the payment to anyone with a high carbon footprint. There is likely to be a public interest issue in making sure that whoever received the payment, did in fact spend it addressing the commitment.

The payment could, perhaps should, go to a fund. A national fund within which there would be many restricted funds, organized by the type of commitment and by whether the commitment was local, national or international. A national trust fund perhaps. As the payment to the fund is not charitable and not a tax, it would need to be arms-length from government. The fund would then make payments to organizations dealing with the relevant commitments.

Similar funds exist already, for example the payments made to a Zakat Foundation in a particular country. These payments represent a commitment and there is an expectation by third parties that the payment will be made; they are a constructive obligation. A new trust fund might follow that same logic, rebuilding trust at the same time, where payments are not a flat percentage but proportionate to the contribution of the harm done. If there is still a concern about estimates, Zakat is based simply on a percentage of relevant assets.[14] A calculation that does not try to relate the amount paid to the contribution of the business to relevant issues. But it works well enough.

Investment managers will move their investments to businesses that do less harm. Good. But in this approach, there would still be no incentive to move investments to those businesses which are also more effective at creating positive changes to well-being. A restriction on doing no harm may not be enough. It may a stepping stone.

Accounting for positive and negative externalities

Looking further ahead then, an accounting system could account for positive changes as well as negative changes to well-being for current and future generations, for positive and negative externalities. This has more challenges, not least accepting that this system could only be defined and developed with a more democratic process and from within a more equitable and inclusive society. Nonetheless, many organizations are already working on this and a long history of cost benefit analysis, social return on investment and impact assessment, providing information alongside financial accounts. There is much to explore, building on this experience, to create parallel accounts, with more sharing of ideas between the two approaches – and it will probably be easier to add positive externalities from a basis where negative externalities are already accounted for. In the same way markets are based on information from people transacting between each other, well-being must be based on information from people. The tendency to short cut this, because it is cheaper, or because 'people do not know what they want' when used by people with more power than those they are talking about, is a slippery slope to 'not well-being accounting'.

This would be a world where everyone has the best chance to live fulfilling lives, where they can buy and sell products and services that contribute to their lives. A market economy, but an economy built on the best of what it is to be human, where our kindness, empathy, creativity, imagination and entrepreneurialism are guiding us towards creating fulfilling lives. A world where resources are still scarce and need to be distributed and allocated to those products and services that best achieve these goals. A competitive market economy serving the public interest. Who'd have thought.

An accounting system that addresses this is more challenging, but public sector accounting could start researching and piloting approaches and provide well-being accounts alongside existing financial accounts, consistent with cost benefit analysis. So, the purpose would be net positive changes to well-being (including the use of money to achieve those changes). This would need another change to paragraph 1.3 in the Conceptual Framework to update the purpose. Paragraph 1.3 would become something like, 'The decisions described in paragraph 1.2 depend on *the change in current and future generations' well-being* that existing and potential investors, lenders and other creditors expect…'.

This might sound all a bit fluffy, even to non-accountants. But well-being was in the IFAC's public interest statement, recognizing that public interest is the net benefits, and included well-being; also, it is in the IPSASB's Conceptual Framework and in the IMF paper on externalities.[15] It has cropped up throughout this book and it is already being used in practice.

This change does raise issues for accounting, some of which were identified in a Capitals Coalition report on 'A Conceptual Framework for Sustainability Reporting' that was based as much as possible on the IFRS Conceptual Framework.[16] One issue relates to a profit and loss account. Information on management's stewardship in the context of well-being will be needed. This would be information on how effectively management has reduced negative and increased positive externalities and made trade-offs between different options with different externalities – and between groups of people, between current and future generations and between different capitals. This goes further now than the comparison between options with different negative consequences as there is also a comparison between positive and negative consequences. This comparison is also implicit when managers choose between options. The investor is going to need to know how managers have made these choices, comparing these different sets of impacts in relation to the resources allocated following a decision, and is fundamental to making information useful. It should not lead to opening a Pandora's box of issues where every action leads to arguments about one group benefiting and another losing. Firstly, a competitive marketplace has winners and losers and, providing markets are free and fair, companies that are not competitive and which close are not considered an externality, though society may still choose to support employees who lose their jobs as a result. Secondly these trade-offs are happening all the time in all business decisions. We just need some new norms to decide which should be recognized – and which should not. The accounting system is the best place to iron this out.

One of the other issues relates to concepts of capital, the last section in the IFRS Conceptual Framework. Considering different types of capital is the closest we're going to get to double-entry bookkeeping. Double entry just means that every transaction can be seen from two perspectives – and both should be recorded. If I buy something I have less money but more of whatever I have bought. As a result of recognizing two sides (a credit for what I have less of and a debit for what I have more of), this approach also provides some level of control; the total of both sides must come to the same total, and balance. When an investor provides money to a business, the business has money, a debit, but also has a liability to repay the investor, a credit. This liability is the capital that was introduced.

Figure 9.1 below sets out the structure of a balance sheet. There are two sides: debits and credits. Equity is the money introduced by the investors, sometimes called the capital introduced. Reserves are the accumulated trading profits and losses. We have become used to

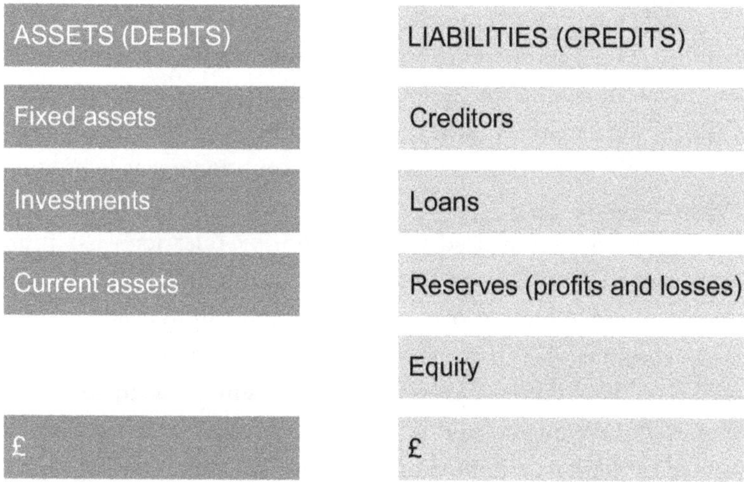

ASSETS (DEBITS)
Fixed assets
Investments
Current assets
£
LIABILITIES (CREDITS)
Creditors
Loans
Reserves (profits and losses)
Equity
£

Figure 9.1: Assets and liabilities

Source: Author

the idea there is one capital in accounting and so only one account for equity. But a different basis for accounting may mean this needs a rethink.

The big challenge is how well-being accounting could recognize positive impacts. These are not owned or controlled by a business so they cannot be assets. If we recognize the positive, and it is not an asset, it will need a new element defined in the Conceptual Framework. And would need to recognize a liability, the double entry, which could be a new form of equity building on the earlier idea for meeting a constructive obligation by issuing shares. If the positive change was to nature, it could mean that nature would become a type of equity holder. This raises questions about the rights of this 'investor', and who represents them. It could mean that the public interest would be redefined and would be represented directly in the board room, proportionately to the dependence of the business model on other capitals. There are many possibilities. When the UK Parliament created limited liability, it recognized a public benefit, but this was only one option. Another would have been creating this investor, representing the public interest and ensuring decisions were being made for investors and the public interest, rather than assuming they were the same. This is not dissimilar to companies in which the government has a Golden Share, a share to which special rights accrue (and another use of 'Golden'). A transition to well-being accounting opens interesting possibilities.

There would also need to be accounting rules for what is an acceptable trade-off between different capitals and when a trade-off is not permitted. A big part of our problems comes from making things commensurate when that are not. For example, making a decision with a trade-off between providing employment and extinction of a species. But we might avoid this using the idea of restricted reserves as used in charity accounting to ensure that funding is only spent on permitted activities.

Investors would get the information that meets their newly defined needs. Businesses would make payments to compensate for negative impacts. Go further and new equity classes protect the public interest and contribute to debates over strategy and business models. They would move their investments, both as principals and agents, to business models that generate financial returns and contribute to well-being – and at a rate in line with expectations and the public interest. Investors would move to businesses that had net positive impacts and lower levels of dependency and a financial return. Human beings' creativity, and our entrepreneurialism, would be unleashed but now it would be seeking business models that contribute to well-being for all.

It would probably need another look at the public interest statements of all the organizations in the accounting system, to reflect that interest in well-being.

Audit

Audit is the icing on the risk-reduction cake. It is not foolproof. It cannot be. The audit should be planned to reduce the level of audit risk to an acceptable level. The risk is that the audit will miss something and provide an opinion that everything meets legal requirements when it does not. Not easy when we are dealing with unknown unknowns. But the overall approach and thinking behind financial audit is excellent.

Changing purpose would increase the scope of accounts and the need for estimates would now be higher. Accounts would include any harm done throughout the value chain. And that may require a different approach to uncertainty in estimating and modelling but should still be based on information obtained from those experiencing harm.[17] The auditor is now going to have to check that the information is complete and accurate within that new level of uncertainty, to the extent that the information influences users' decisions. This needs some new skills in applying existing concepts.

If assurance is not acting in the interest of the people whose lives are impacted, assurance will not increase accountability. Before International Standard on Sustainability Assurance (ISSA) 5000 was released, the IAASB already provided 'Guidance on Assurance of External Extended Reporting',[18] which addressed types of non-financial reporting including integrated, sustainability and ESG reporting. Paragraph 145 states, 'There may be circumstances when the stakeholders and intended users are not the same. When a stakeholder is not an intended user, their interests may be taken into account by other parties who are intended users.'

This is good, though 'must be taken into account' would have been better, if hard to say in a guidance document. Otherwise, there is a risk that negative consequences to stakeholders' human rights might not be deemed useful information in the context of a scope for a 'sustainability' reporting standard. Anything less would just be another layer of green/impact/SDG 'washing', despite being carried out with the best of intentions. This is also an issue for maintaining a three-party relationship between those who prepare, use and audit the information, with the auditor acting in the interests of, and reporting to, the user. How can the auditor report to anyone who has, let alone might, experience changes in their well-being? But with a change in purpose the auditor is reporting to the same defined user who now has an interest in what happens to others. This is implicit in other standards and legislation, for example those UN Guiding Principles for Business and Human Rights and in the European Commission's Corporate Sustainability Due Diligence Directive.[19]

There will inevitably be some variation between how directors identify and construct obligations for harm being done. Until the late twentieth century, mining companies' disclosure of the closure costs of mines was voluntary and variable. As accounting standards were introduced, initial uncertainty and variability on the detail of how these liabilities should be calculated and disclosed was resolved over a few years. The push and pull between mining companies and their auditors and a growing body of examples of disclosure reduced variability while maintaining context-specific judgements.

At least initially, this change would make things more difficult for the auditor and create cost for some businesses, in meeting the public interest. The organizations involved, for example PIOB, would need to consider how governance would evolve to represent views of people experiencing harm. And for those people to have a direct means to hold the PIOB to account.

Accounting for positive and negative externalities does raise some additional issues but work can still progress, alongside an accounting system that accounts for an expectation of financial returns and doing no harm.

Chapter 10

How are we going to change it?

It can be done

We only need to do three things. We need to change a couple of words in the IFRS Conceptual Framework for the private sector, add an accounting standard for public sector accounts to reflect the purpose set out in the IPSASB Conceptual Framework and update some public interest statements. Should be easy enough. Couple of quick phone calls and job done. And it may not even need any new legislation. Which is just as well, as I can't see the streets being full of people shouting 'What do we want? *A change in the basis of accounting standards*. When do we want it? *Now*!'

We cannot expect the current managers of capital markets, increasingly caught between public interest and the interests of the very wealthy, to sort this out. There is no surprise that there has been some focus on climate and less on other SDGs, as even the wealthy realize that climate change just might affect their lives too. But it is going to have to be representatives of all people, acting in everyone's interests, to sort out the other SDGs. Not just the few, living in a la la land of an economic system where maximizing private wealth leaves any other consequences to be resolved by personal ethics and public taxes.

This might be a bit harder now that there is the ISSB and those responsible for the accounting system can argue that they have all this sustainability stuff covered. The IASB has considered the effect of climate change on the accounts in additional educational material[1] and includes examples to improve climate-related reporting.[2] And yes, the IFRS established the ISSB to consider sustainability-related financial disclosures. But these do not consider or change the fundamental basis for which costs are included and which are excluded. There is so much noise out there about non-financial, or sustainability, or ESG reporting. No one, or only a very few, talk about financial reporting in the context of sustainability. A contribution to water pollution may have a negative effect on a local community's health or reduce the availability of fish. It could also affect a company's future operating costs if there is an expectation of the industry being charged under polluter pays legislation. If this is reported in a sustainability report, it may well also need to be added to the financial statements for them to give a true and fair view.

Although no change to international accounting standards is required, the change to purpose in the IFRS Conceptual Framework would have implications for how they are applied. Those countries that have mandated IASB standards would want to agree to a revised Conceptual Framework if this had significant implications, so there will be a job to do to get buy-in. It would require a change to the interpretation of what is true and fair or how accounting bodies are meeting the public interest, which would also need broad legal and political acceptance. But the basis is already there. This is not introducing something new; it is amending something that exists.

Getting to the point that governments support those changes requires evidence that they are possible, and desired. There will be those who do not want change, perhaps those whose own wealth and power would be affected. There will be those who will explain that accounting wasn't designed to do that. They may not 'mansplain', but they will 'powersplain' and tell us why change is not possible, why only the proposals of those with power understand what changes are needed and are possible. Why including these costs would bring about disaster – as if not including these costs is not already a disaster. But empowerment means giving up power, it means giving up control of the narrative that had maintained power. Sustainability is more than climate and more than nature. It includes social justice and equality, and inequality affects us all and we all live less fulfilling lives in a world where the economic system engenders inequality. Fixing for climate while ignoring how profit is calculated might be possible, but it isn't sustainable development.

Stage 1: Voluntary

This is the proof-of-concept stage, showing that it is possible for businesses to account for many of the consequences of their business models and to do this within existing accounting standards and existing legislation. This is up to directors, plus anyone who has some influence over them – and there are a slowly growing number of examples. A broader range covering different sustainability issues, in different parts of the world, would be enough to support the concept.

Why would directors want to voluntarily add information to their accounts, let alone make commitments that recognize a responsibility to pay for the impacts of their business? Perhaps the main reason is if they conclude that the information is necessary to give a true and fair view, so that they are meeting their legal duty! As George Bompas KC said at the end of his opinion,[3] 'Directors need to exert themselves and cannot simply delegate to others.'

They might want to construct an obligation because they think it will speed up the rate at which they make decisions and reduce costs that are likely to increase in future, reducing the risks to which their business model contributes. If they are the owners, they may simply want to be responsible. It cannot be responsible, or ethical, to book profits that come with unaccounted-for costs, only not recognized because the people experiencing those costs have little or no chance of accessing and gaining compensation.

Or they might do it because they care. Directors might protect themselves from the company breaching its civil law duty of care by taking effective steps to ensure that all relevant employees receive the right training to recognize harm and support an effective grievance process to raise instances of harm. Directors might then want to consider whether any harm done to current or future generations is aligned with that company duty of care or aligned with the UN Guiding Principles on Business and Human Rights.

Although recognizing these costs may be uncomfortable, it should be at least equally uncomfortable to ignore them. And it is not that hard. Accounts can already include accounting estimates *and* be based on models. Whether your estimates and your valuations of these obligations are good enough to be true and fair is a discussion between the directors and their auditor. If you want to rise above the challenges of sustainability reporting, just start by estimating those obligations. This will very quickly force those boardroom discussions on how to remove them and quickly drill these down to managers' decisions at all levels. It would operationalize risks overnight, including sustainability related risks.

Recognizing these costs now is arguably necessary for a business' resilience and competitiveness. It could reduce, for example, a dependency on access to clean water or related insurance becomes more expensive,[4] and an impact, if polluting water increases the risk of higher future liabilities.[5] Legislation and social norms are slowly catching up. Better to bite the bullet now. Leave it too late and it will be just that, too late.

Stage 2: Encouraging

Well, we all need a little help doing what's right. This stage provides further proof of the concept by showing it is possible for some users. This might be investors, or perhaps businesses buying from others or governments own commissioning of products and services, who expect information on these consequences to be disclosed in financial reports, covering both notes and commitments that give rise to liabilities.

Why would investors want to see these costs recognized and lower their returns? Investors, especially those very large investors – those with billions if not trillions under investment – face different risks. Arguably they are so large and portfolios are so diversified that they face risks that run across the whole market and cannot be diversified away. They are what was referred to as 'universal owners' in Chapter 2.

Investors have been increasingly concerned about the issue of systemic risk. Systemic risks result from the accumulation of negative externalities in the economy and are not included in existing financial accounts. If they are relevant, for example, there are potential costs arising from managers' decisions that have not been included, negatively affecting the economic and financial systems, they may need to be disclosed. But if the risk that a business will have to pay these costs is too uncertain for the cost may not be disclosed. And yet the scale of these risks has been increasing, and are of increasing concern to universal owners, affecting their view of what information matters, or what is 'material'. Investors need to feed their expectations through to accountants and auditors. Some investors – whether diversified or not – may also be impact investors; they invest with the specific aim of creating positive impacts and may have a particular focus. These investors could also encourage directors to consider the relevant consequences of their business model.

Stage 3: Mandatory

Practical examples can then inform both public debate and the legal arguments needed to support a shift from a voluntary to an expected recognition of costs. Five things, perhaps more, perhaps fewer, are required, involving standard setters and regulators, but needing government mandate.

First, consistency between the public interest in aligning social and private returns (and so no externalities) and the (mainly existing) public interest statements of accounting bodies and financial reporting and auditing practice, which result in externalities by allowing costs to be excluded.

Second, a clear statement reinterpreting the true and fair requirement so that accounts cannot give a true and fair view unless directors have constructed obligations for the consequences of their business model. In countries where company legislation does not have a true and fair requirement, it might be necessary to put this requirement in accounting standards, for example as New Zealand has done with NZ IAS1.[6]

Third, government to be reinstated as a primary user of financial reports within the IFRS Conceptual Framework. Governments have a wider expectation than financial returns, plus a role to act in the interests of those experiencing the consequences of investments. They could raise this through their membership of IOSCO and broaden IOSCO membership to include a wider range of regulators.

Fourth, mandate a change to the purpose behind financial reporting, as this sets the scene for how all accounts would be prepared. Getting a change to the basis of financial reporting is based on the argument that the existing basis does not reflect the expectations of the maximum number of users – i.e., the interest in financial returns and nothing else – for either the existing group of primary users or for the largest, but excluded, user of financial statements. At a minimum, the IASB may want to reassess the assumption that the expectation of the maximum number of primary users is financial returns and nothing else using a consultation process that is representative of primary users. A wider public debate would highlight the inconsistency, and governments may want to raise the issue with their representatives on the IOSCO.

Finally, a requirement for a public accounting standard on well-being accounting, to be consistent with the IPSASB Conceptual Framework where the purpose of government is to maintain and enhance well-being.

Some governments may be more supportive than others. The UN declaration[7] following the 2025 Finance for Development conference in Sevilla made it clear that the international financial system needs reform and needs to internalize externalities.

Transition to mandatory

There will need to be a transition. It will not be possible to shift overnight from no businesses recognizing these costs to all businesses recognizing all these costs. Deciding how to manage the transition will need help from civil society as much as accountants, lawyers and politicians. All these voices have ideas, experience and knowledge that can make this happen. For now, just a few ideas could include the following.

1. Start with disclosing information on externalities and related risks, the impacts and dependencies, as a note to the accounts, showing the amount of harm and the cost. Businesses that are already separately disclosing sustainability information could use this as a starting point. The note would then fall under existing audit requirements and quickly drive standardization. It would also encourage accounting software companies to produce solutions for different impacts and dependencies.
2. Start with a requirement for directors to consider whether they decided to create constructive obligations and include their decision in the directors' report. Users might conclude that, where directors had decided not to construct an obligation for their contribution to externalities, the business could not be described as a responsible business.
3. Start with some impacts and then move to others, informed by the SDGs, perhaps moving through climate, gender, nature and decent work. This would happen naturally as, with experience, the quality of information collected reaches a level that can be disclosed in financial statements.
4. Incentivize businesses, for example, by making it a requirement for public commissioning, where the link to a public interest that is wider than financial returns is implicit, and is mirrored in many public sector best value procurement requirements.
5. Use broader estimates and models for impacts of smaller businesses, perhaps by sector. This might have more push back but if the balance is shifting to the public interest and given there are examples like Zakat which use a broad percentage of relevant assets, this could work.
6. Use a minimum level, which could vary, for recognition of the costs as opposed to disclosure in the notes.
7. Follow the logic used in greenhouse gas accounting of Scope 1, 2 and 3 for other impacts and dependencies and start with the equivalent of scope 1 and 2. In greenhouse gas

accounting, scope 1 addresses emissions from sources controlled by the company and scope 2 covers indirect emissions from purchased energy. Scope 3 covers everything else in the supply chain and the use of products. If all businesses accounted for costs for scope 1 and 2 as a constructive obligation, the level of scope 3, would significantly reduce.

What could you do to make this happen?

There is always something. Exactly what depends on who you are. And what timescale you are acting over. We'll need a bit of everything to turn the ship around. These are just some ideas to get us all talking and doing.

Investors

As a private investor investing through your pension, investment trusts or another saving scheme you could:

- write to your investment or fund manager, or your pension fund, and tell them that you are not only interested in financial returns but also the social and environmental consequences of those returns. You do not want your investments to do harm to others.
- ask them:
    - How you can be sure your investments are aligned with this interest?
    - How does the investment manager know that investee accounts give a true and fair view?

As a private investor investing directly you could start by asking investee companies these questions.

- How has the organization considered the requirement for financial statements to give a true and fair view in the context of increasing business risks, including sustainability?
- Was the board discussion recorded and minuted?

- If the investee makes claims to be a responsible business but has decided not to take responsibility for costs relating to its negative impacts, how do they justify this decision and align it with their claim to be a responsible business?

As a universal owner (of equity investments) you could:

- make it clear that the scale and cost of a businesses' contribution to systemic risks is material to your use of the financial statements;
- ask auditors whether they were considering what additional information might be required in order for the accounts to give a true and fair view;
- engage with asset managers, companies, investment advisors, governments, standard setters, ratings agencies to encourage them to follow your lead;
- model systemic risks in financial analysis and consider them in investment belief and policy statements; and
- adjust investment team incentives to consider externalities.

As an investment manager you could:

- ask investors, whether they have expectations relating to social and environmental returns or to investments where companies manage and disclose information on any harm resulting from the business model;
- ask investors in addition for information on financial risk preferences – what are their risk preferences for negative consequences for others?

Company directors

You could:

- review how you concluded that your accounts gave a true and fair view and read, or reread;
    - SVI's international or country specific guidance on 'Are your Accounts True and Fair';

- the FRC guidance on true and fair[8] or equivalent in your jurisdiction; and
- the latest international legal opinions and research, for example the UK legal opinion;[9]

- ask for a summary of the above at the next board meeting so all directors get the information;
- review existing sustainability or ESG disclosures and consider whether any of these should be included as notes in the financial statements to give a true and fair view;
- identify one or two of the negative consequences (or impacts) of running the business that are not already in the financial statements;
- advocate for changes to create a level playing field for all businesses to disclose information on their contribution to externalities;
- realize that your profits may be being made at someone else's cost and that this amounts to avoiding an obligation only because you can, and consider if this has implications for the company's duty of care;
- discuss, decide and record whether to accept responsibility for any of these costs in line with a duty to promote success of the business;
- take minutes of any board discussion, prior to approving the accounts, on whether additional information should be disclosed for the accounts to give a true and fair view, noting the reasons for your decisions and the weight given to competing factors.

Financial Directors and Chief Financial Officers (well, any other accountants)

You could refer to all that guidance the other directors are reading listed above and consider:

- if you would propose adding other information to the accounts to give a true and fair view;

- how you would advise the directors if they ask you anything about their legal duty;
- the pros and cons of creating a constructive obligation;
- whether the risk register reflects the relevant risks arising from impacts and dependencies of the business model;
- how the financial value of the consequences of the risks are assessed and reported.

In addition to thinking about additional information in the accounts and possible constructive obligations you could consider:

- reading the UNDP SDG Impact Standards and supporting materials and the UNDP/ISO SDG Management Standard;
- putting in a system to collect information on the consequences of decisions;
- providing decision makers with information to help them understand the trade-offs they may be making;
- reading some of the work on Impact Profit and Loss accounts as a way of reporting the aggregation of all these trade-offs;
- joining groups working on this and sharing with your professional networks.

Auditors

You could:

- double check whether the company said anything in public that might have created a valid expectation in third parties that a responsibility has been accepted, and a payment will be made;
- consider whether further guidance from your firm's technical department, your professional body, or from the relevant regulatory bodies on these issues would be useful.

Legal and risk – general counsels, in house legal teams, external counsel and risk and compliance officers

You could:

- consider whether the directors have complied with their duty to only approve accounts that give a true and fair view and considered whether additional information would be necessary to give that view;
- consider whether decisions made that may have led to 'externalized' social or environmental costs are appropriate;
- consider whether the business has made claims that are consistent with a decision not to accept responsibility for the costs of the consequences of the business model;
- consider whether the terms of engagement with the auditors been sufficiently clear on the requirements for the accounts to give a true and fair view;
- consider whether the terms of directors' service or employment agreements are reinforced with appropriate guidance in relation to directors' duties (including, if relevant, the true and fair requirement, the duty of care, the duty to promote the success of the company);
- ensure directors receive training to ensure they have the necessary competencies for their role.

Employees

You could:

- have a look at your organization's accounts and whether the organization discloses its contribution to externalities;
- raise the question in team and staff meetings;
- if you are changing job this could be one of the questions you ask in an interview, for example, has the company considered making commitments that would construct an obligation relating to its impacts and managing risks of dependencies.

Economics and business school students

You want to change the world. You have a microeconomics course coming. You could:

- ask how this economic model determines which costs get included and why;
- ask what alternative models exist and what these would mean for accounts;
- ask what is the cause of externalities;
- ask about legally enforceable and constructive obligations and the link with externalities.

Accounting students

If you do want to change the world, see the previous list. If you are also interested in getting a job in accounting, you could:

- check that your course equips you for the growing questions in connectivity between risk, sustainability and financial reporting;
- check that you have had a lecture on the true and fair requirement and directors' duty to only approve accounts that are true and fair. If not, ask for one – and make sure that it covers:
  - the links between directors' duties and the financial accounts;
  - the implications of being a purpose led organizations for the true and fair requirement (as might arise in the UK from Companies Act s172 (2));
  - examples of when conformity with accounting standards did not result in accounts that gave a true and fair view.

Accounting tutor and lecturers

You could:

- do the same as for students, before they ask the questions. But don't expect to have all the answers;

- campaign for inclusion of modules that educate around the issues of sustainability and help equip students with the skills to understand key issues. In the UK, the ICAEW now has a sustainability course which is being piloted by the University of Liverpool with first year accounting students.

Civil society and foundations

If your work seeks to address inequality and reduce power imbalances in society, you could consider whether your work considers the role of financial accounting in creating the problems you want to address. For example, Friends Provident Foundation[10] in the UK states:

> We believe that the way our economy operates causes many of the problems that we face in society, but it does not have to be this way. We have a vision for a better economy that will serve society and planet instead of extracting from it. Since we were established, we have focused on money, the economy and how they link to society. We believe we need to take a systems change approach to the economy, challenging the structures, power dynamics and beliefs that keep it operating as it currently does.

Or perhaps like Oxfam[11]

> A huge concentration of global corporate and monopoly power is exacerbating inequality economy-wide. Seven out of ten of the world's biggest corporates have either a billionaire CEO or a billionaire as their principal shareholder. Through squeezing workers, dodging tax, privatizing the state and spurring climate breakdown, corporations are driving inequality and acting in the service of delivering ever-greater wealth to their rich owners. To end extreme inequality, governments must radically redistribute the power of billionaires and corporations back to ordinary people. A more equal world is possible if governments effectively regulate and reimagine the private sector.

Public policy – politicians, advisors, think tanks

Financial accounting may seem somewhat arcane when you are working on health, housing, transport or education. But hopefully you may now want to consider the role that our accounting system has played in contributing to those challenges. You could:

- ask who is your representative on IOSCO and what is their remit;
- consider how you ensure that the institutions that manage and support the economy have public interest statements that refer to aligning private and social costs and returns;
- consider how you ensure that those institutions then act in accordance with that public interest statement;
- consider whether you are comfortable that the accounting system produces audited accounts that reflect the public interest;
- consider whether you are able to compare the projected costs and benefits of government funded policies or programmes with the actual costs and benefits achieved;
- consider whether the benefits in those reports tied back to changes in well-being;
- consider whether the statements of benefits included are limited to intended benefits.

If you work for a financial regulator, given the gravity of the issues around the accounting system, the scale of the people affected and the financial and other losses experienced, you could consider whether there is a public interest issue.

Voters and many of the above

Even if you are not a finance director or an auditor you may be able to talk to one. There are, after all, approximately 3,000,000 accountants worldwide. Many are also finance directors. And approximately 600,000 are auditors.

We may feel powerless, especially in between elections. But an MPs post box influences policy. You could email or write to ask your MP whether:

- they have considered whether there are human rights risks or environmental risks arising from the application of financial accounting standards;
- they have considered the role the accounting system plays in creating externalities;
- whether their policies increase or reduce well-being and whether they can provide any evidence;
- they are going to require public sector accounts to include information on service performance in increasing or maintaining well-being.

We need a much wider public debate on users, expenditure, externalities, public interest, and truth and fairness. Despite appearances, the accounting system should be working in the public interest. It may seem boring, but that is its superpower – its cloak of invisibility.

Conclusion

Our world is either burning or flooding, the challenges seem insurmountable and time is running out. It might seem that the most sensible reaction is to go out and party.

We need to start by understanding the problem and then imagining a different world. Not though by trying to predict what products and services we'll all be using in 2100. History is littered with examples of our individual inability to predict the level of detail that results from the ideas of billions of people – except, of course, for *Star Trek*'s prediction that we would all have communicators. Look what happens if you try to be specific. Howard Aiken, the builder of the Mark 1 calculator, is reputed to have said in 1948 – 'I think there is a world market for maybe five computers'. We need to imagine a world built on better principles.

The pilots of that Air France flight (see the introduction to part 1) didn't have enough time to work out the problem, let alone a solution. We have more time. The problem is not implicit in a market economy, far from it, and it is not about human greed, which is only one aspect of human behaviour, nor is it even accounting in general as we do need to be held to account for our actions. It is the purpose of financial accounting and the limit on which costs are recognized when profits are calculated. A business's transactions create costs that are not included in the calculation of profit. Costs that can exceed the profits being made.

It is only 50 years since the first international accounting standard and only 36 since the first conceptual framework to guide the application of standards. Such a short time to have locked down an approach to recognizing cost that is causing so much unintended damage. The solution is not to try and legislate against actions that cause those costs, or raise taxes to address the damage, or make future plans to do less damage. Though all of these might help. The solution must be to change the way profit is calculated, and then rely on human creativity, imagination and entrepreneurialism to create and respond to a new measure of profit that plays to what is best in being human: our ability to be kind, to consider others and create joy. Hopefully, this book shows that it is possible and how we all have a part to play in creating the accounting system we need.

Our accounting system can keep the same decisions, those economic decisions to provide resources to organizations. And the same primary users, so long as we add one other user, government, receiving and spending taxes in the public interest. But we need to change the expectation of those users to include an interest in what happens to people and to our planet alongside any financial returns. We can keep the same accounting standards, with those constructive obligations becoming a requirement for accounts to be true and fair and meet the public interest.

There probably needs to be change in governance as well, especially as a friend of mine told me I would have 'Jeremy loves governance' written on my tombstone. Although it is up to countries to adopt international accounting standards and although IOSCO's members represent governments, I still think that capital markets and the accounting system should work within an international treaty and be part of the United Nations, designed and able to represent the voices of all of us who gain and lose from that system, and to recognize and address disagreements, with the Golden Rule at its heart. This would allow us to continue the journey towards well-being accounting for current and future generations.

As I have said before, there is much to love in the IFRS Conceptual Framework for Financial Reporting and it seems fitting to end with a reference. Paragraph 1.11 says:

> As with most goals, the Conceptual Framework's vision of ideal financial reporting is unlikely to be achieved in full, at least not in the short term, because it takes time to understand, accept and implement new ways of analysing transactions and other events. Nevertheless, establishing a goal towards which to strive is essential if financial reporting is to evolve so as to improve its usefulness.

Exactly. The accounting system does need to change, but it can. These 'other events' include the impacts arising from transactions, leading to externalities and the growing gap between private and social costs and returns. If we close that gap, entrepreneurs and innovators will carry on, but with ideas that create value for customers and investors that do not depend on taking value from other citizens. If we do not, profits will be made, costs will continue to be imposed, and the damage will become catastrophic.

Photograph of a wall in Princes Avenue, Liverpool

Source: Author

Notes

Part 1: The problem: Why accounting is damaging society

1. www.popularmechanics.com/flight/airlines/a45250041/what-really-happened-aboard-air-france-447/ (Accessed 15 April 2025.)

2. www.imf.org/-/media/Files/Publications/WP/2023/English/wpiea2023169-print-pdf.ashx (Accessed 6 August 2025.)

3. https://capitalscoalition.org/publication/unpriced-environmental-costs-the-top-externalities-of-the-global-market-report/ (Accessed 7 October 2025.) The negative externalities relate to air pollution, greenhouse gases, land use, water, water and land pollution and water use.

4. In 2018, ILO estimated unpaid care work at US$11 trillion, though this will not all be attributable to business. International Labour Organization. Care Work and Care Jobs for the Future of Decent Work. Geneva, International Labour Office, 2018, p. 43. www.ilo.org/global/publications/books/WCMS_633135/lang--en/index.htm (Accessed 8 August 2025.)

5. Doll, Richard, and A. Bradford Hill. 'Smoking and Carcinoma of the Lung: Preliminary Report.' *British Medical Journal*, vol. 2, no. 4682, 1950, pp. 739–748. www.bmj.com/content/2/4682/739

6. https://exposetobacco.org/news/tobacco-industry-lies/ (Accessed 26 August 2025.)

7. www.documentcloud.org/documents/3227654-PSAC-1965-Restoring-the-Quality-of-Our-Environment/ (Accessed 26 August 2025.)

8. www.brownlawyers.ca/asbestos/who-knew-asbestos-was-dangerous-and-when/?utm (Accessed 26 August 2025.)

9. For a longer discussion of the Golden Rule, see Gensler, Hatty J., *Ethics and the Golden Rule*, Routledge, 2018.

10. Parliament of the World's Religions. *Towards a Global Ethic: An Initial Declaration*. 2020 update, Parliament of the World's Religions, 2023.

https://parliamentofreligions.org/wp-content/uploads/2023/05/Global-Ethic-PDF-2020-Update.pdf (Accessed 12 August 2025.)

11 www.learnalberta.ca/content/aswt/indigenous_pedagogy/documents/worldviews_aboriginal_culture.pdf (Accessed 3 August 2025.)

12 New Zealand Government, Manaakitanga Principle. www.digital.govt.nz/standards-and-guidance/privacy-security-and-risk/privacy/data-protection-and-use-policy-dpup/read-the-dpup-principles/manaakitanga-principle (Accessed 12 August 2025.)

Chapter 1: Financial accounting and the mess we are in

1 https://theconversation.com/gdp-is-an-outdated-way-of-measuring-the-health-of-the-economy-it-doesnt-reflect-the-health-of-people-or-the-planet-240810 (Accessed 17 August 2025.)

2 Our World in Data, based on World Bank & Maddison (2017). OurWorldInData.org/economic-growth. Licensed under CC BY 4.0.

3 These levels are set by the World Bank. US$6.85 is the poverty threshold for upper middle-income countries. US$2.16 is the threshold for extreme poverty.

4 Maddison, Angus. *Contours of the World Economy, 1–2030 AD: Essays in Macro-Economic History*. Oxford University Press, 2007.

5 www.imf.org/external/datamapper/NGDPD@WEO/OEMDC/ADVEC/WEOWORLD (Accessed 12 August 2025.)

6 www.sapiens.org/archaeology/life-expectancy-measure-misperception/ (Accessed 12 August 2025.)

7 https://ourworldindata.org/life-expectancy?utm_source (Accessed 12 August 2025.)

8 It has fallen a little between 2019 and 2021.

9 https://data.unicef.org/topic/child-survival/under-five-mortality/?utm (Accessed 12 August 2025.)

10 As ever, causality should not be assumed. Given the main drivers of the increase in life expectancy it may be possible to achieve that goal on a much lower GDP. In 2023 Vietnam's life expectancy was over 70 with a GDP per head of just over US$4,000 and in 2022, Cuba's was over 80 with a GDP per head of just over US$9,000.

11 https://ons.gov.uk/peoplepopulationandcommunity/healthandsocialcare/healthinequalities/bulletins/healthstatelifeexpectanciesbyindexofmultipledeprivationimd/2018to2020 (Accessed 12 August 2025.)

12 https://worldpopulationreview.com/country-rankings/life-expectancy-by-country?utm (Accessed 16 May 2025.)

13 www.johnstonsarchive.net/other/worldpop.html (Accessed 12 August 2025.)

14 https://database.earth/population/by-country/2025 (Accessed 12 August 2025.)

15 www.worldbank.org/en/publication/poverty-and-shared-prosperity (Accessed 12 August 2025.)

16 www.nature.com/articles/s41467-025-56906-7?utm (Accessed 12 August 2025.)

17 *The Oxford Handbook of Ethics and Economics*, Chapter 16 'The Moral Status of Profit'. Oxford University Press, 2019.

18 www.theguardian.com/environment/2014/sep/04/bp-18bn-extra-fines-us-ruling-gulf-of-mexico-oil-spill-deepwater-horizon-reckless?utm (Accessed 12 August 2025.)

19 https://masgc.org/oilscience/NAS-Pre-Workshop-Summary.FINAL.pdf?utm (Accessed 12 August 2025.)

20 www.personneltoday.com/hr/birmingham-city-council-to-settle-6000-equal-pay-claims (Accessed 16 May 2025.)

21 See the Capital Coalition's Protocols for examples of other dependencies. capitalscoalition.org/capitals-approach/natural-capital-protocol/?fwp_filter_tabs=guide_supplement

22 https://insights.aib.world/article/90323-_imagine-a-better-world_-an-interview-with-paul-polman-aib-2023-international-executive-of-the-year? (Accessed 24 September 2025.)

23 www.nbcnews.com/news/nbcblk/calls-reparations-are-old-emancipation-will-global-powers-finally-list-rcna9800 (Accessed 16 May 2025.)

24 https://ourworldindata.org/economic-inequality-by-gender (Accessed 16 May 2025.)

25 Mobutu Sese Seko, 25 November 1977, in a speech cited by D. J. Gould in 'Patrons and Clients: The Role of the Military in Zaire Politics' in Isaac Mowoe (ed.), *The Performance of Soldiers as Governors*. University Press of America, p. 485.

26 www.contagious.com/news-and-views/hellmanns-terry-smith-and-the-paradox-of-purposeful-brands (Accessed 12 August 2025.)

Chapter 2: How have we managed to miss this?

1 Carney, Mark. 'How We Get What We Value.' The Reith Lectures, BBC Radio 4, 2 December 2020. www.bbc.co.uk/programmes/m000py8t (Accessed 12 August 2025.)

2 www.economicshelp.org/blog/glossary/externalities/ (Accessed 16 May 2025.)

3 Coase, Ronald H. 'The Problem of Social Cost.' *Journal of Law and Economics*, vol. 3, 1960, pp. 1–44.

4 www.imf.org/en/Publications/fandd/issues/Series/Back-to-Basics/Externalities (Accessed 16 May 2025.)

5 www.investopedia.com/ask/answers/032315/what-difference-between-accounting-and-economics.asp (Accessed 12 August 2025.)

6 Smith, Adam. *An Inquiry into the Nature and Causes of the Wealth of Nations*. Edited by Edwin Cannan. Modern Library, 1994.

7 Cooper, David J. and Michael J. Sherer. 'The Value of Corporate Accounting Reports: Arguments for a Political Economy of Accounting.' *Accounting, Organizations and Society*, vol. 9, no. 3–4, 1984, pp. 207–232.

[8] Sahan, Erinch, et al. 'What Doughnut Economics Means for Business: Creating Enterprises That Are Regenerative and Distributive by Design.' Doughnut Economics Action Lab, November 2022.

[9] www.mckinsey.com/industries/financial-services/our-insights/global-payments-in-2024-simpler-interfaces-complex-reality?utm (Accessed 12 August 2025.)

[10] www.theguardian.com/news/datablog/2012/may/24/robert-kennedy-gdp (Accessed 14 April 2025.)

[11] www.ons.gov.uk/economy/grossdomesticproductgdp/articles/whatis gdp/2016-11-21 (Accessed 14 April 2025.)

[12] This is another reference to well-being. It will keep coming up, so it is time for a definition. The international standard, Governance of Organisations – Developing Indicators for Effective Governance, defines well-being as a: *'positive state of being where people's needs are met, such that they have the capacity and opportunity to lead fulfilling lives'* and notes that *'Well-being is also referred to as a state of flourishing or a 'good life'.*

[13] Commission on the Measurement of Economic Performance and Social Progress. Report by the Commission on the Measurement of Economic Performance and Social Progress. OECD Publishing, 2009.

[14] https://blogs.cfainstitute.org/marketintegrity/2021/05/03/esg-qa-moving-beyond-modern-portfolio-theory/?utm_source=chatgpt.com (Accessed 3 August 2025.)

[15] www.takingcharge.csh.umn.edu/can-money-buy-happiness (Accessed 8 February 2025.)

[16] https://abcnews.go.com/Business/judge-rejected-elon-musks-50-billion-tesla-pay/story?id=116403271 (Accessed 12 August 2025.)

[17] www.kcl.ac.uk/news/wealth-inequality-risks-triggering-societal-colla pse-within-next-decade-report-finds (Accessed 12 August 2025.)

[18] Diamond, Jared M. *Why is Sex Fun?: The Evolution of Human Sexuality*. HarperCollins, 1997 (1st edn).

[19] *The Oxford Handbook of Ethics and Economics*, Chapter 8 'On the Evolution of Ethics, Rationality and Economic Behaviour. Oxford University Press, 2019.

20 www.youtube.com/watch?v=NAOQH4xEyhM (Accessed 29 January 2025.)

21 www.comedy.co.uk/live/shows/625/stewart-lee-41st-best-stand-up/?utm (Accessed 29 August 2025.)

22 https://scrapsfromtheloft.com/comedy/stewart-lee-content-provider-transcript/ (Accessed 29 January 2025.)

23 Take one example from the FRC's auditing standard on Materiality in Planning and Performing an Audit from paragraph 4, '*In this context, it is reasonable for the auditor to assume that users: … (d) Make reasonable economic decisions on the basis of the information in the financial statements.*'

24 Saad, Aisha I. and Diane Strauss. 'The New "Reasonable Investor" and Changing Frontiers of Materiality: Increasing Investor Reliance on ESG Disclosures and Implications for Securities Litigation.' *Berkeley Business Law Journal*, vol. 17, no. 2, 2020, pp. 391–433.

25 https://reports.weforum.org/docs/WEF_Global_Risks_Report_2025.)pdf (Accessed 8 August, 2025.)

26 Edelman Trust Institute. 2025 Edelman Trust Barometer: Global Report. Edelman, January 2025. www.edelman.com/sites/g/files/aatuss191/files/2025-01/2025%20Edelman%20Trust%20Barometer_Final.pdf

27 www.ohchr.org/sites/default/files/Documents/Publications/GuidingPrinciplesBusinessHR_EN.pdf

28 The IFRS carries out regular public consultations, following a formal process set out in the *Due Process Handbook*. Consultation responses are primarily received from agents, acting on behalf of their principals. In the run up to establishing the ISSB, the IFRS carried out a public consultation that received over 500 responses. The vast majority were from finance organizations, accounting bodies, academics and industry. In general, from agents not from principals.

29 https://eur-lex.europa.eu/eli/reg/2024/3015/oj/eng (Accessed 12 August 2025.)

30 Also, by some foreign companies in Japan, by some Canadian companies also listed in the US and by some Israeli companies with a dual listing.

31 www.ifrs.org/about-us/who-we-are/?utm (Accessed 12 August 2025.)

32 www.ifrs.org/groups/ifrs-interpretations-committee/ (Accessed 12 August 2025.)

33 International Sustainability Related Financial Disclosures Board.

34 www.iosco.org/v2/about/?subsection=about_iosco (Accessed 12 August 2025.)

35 www.europarl.europa.eu/RegData/etudes/STUD/2015/542195/IPOL_STU%282015%29542195_EN.pdf?utm (Accessed 12 August 2025.)

36 Marcacci, Antonio. *Transnational Securities Regulation: How It Works, Who Shapes It*. Springer, 2023.

37 www.ifrs.org/groups/monitoring-board/ (Accessed 12 August 2025.)

38 www.iosco.org/library/resolutions/pdf/IOSCORES67.pdf?utm (Accessed 12 August 2025.)

39 www.ipsasb.org/ (Accessed 12 August 2025.)

40 www.ethicsandaudit.org/about (Accessed 12 August 2025.)

41 www.iaasb.org/ (Accessed 12 August 2025.)

42 www.ethicsboard.org/iesba-code (Accessed 12 August 2025.)

43 https://ipiob.org/about/ (Accessed 12 August 2025.)

44 www.ethicsandaudit.org/stakeholder-advisory-council (Accessed 12 August 2025.)

45 www.iosco.org/v2/about/?subsection=monitoring_group (Accessed 12 August 2025.)

46 www.iosco.org/about/monitoring_group/pdf/monitoring-group-statement-on-governance-and-feedback-statement.pdf (Accessed 12 August 2025.)

47 www.iosco.org/about/monitoring_group/pdf/2020-07-MG-Paper-Strengthening-The-International-Audit-And-Ethics-Standard-Setting-System.pdf (Accessed 12 August 2025.)

48 www.intosai.org/ (Accessed 12 August 2025.)

49 www.ifac.org/ (Accessed 12 August 2025.)

50 www.alrc.gov.au/publication/serious-invasions-of-privacy-in-the-digital-era-dp-80/8-balancing-privacy-with-other-interests/meaning-of-public-interest/ (Accessed 12 August 2025.)

51 https://ico.org.uk/for-organisations/foi/freedom-of-information-and-environmental-information-regulations/the-public-interest-test/?utm (Accessed 12 August 2025.)

52 The Institute of Chartered Accountants of England and Wales (ICAEW), the professional body for chartered accountants in the UK, and a member of IFAC, has an excellent framework for analysing public interest 'Acting in the public interest: a framework for analysis'. The framework, as developed by ICAEW's Market Foundations thought leadership programme and, is designed to be used 'in respect of proposals which may be, or have been, justified as being in the public interest. It takes a distinctive view of public interest validity as drawing on a pattern of behaviour that builds up reputation over time, as well as information directly relevant to the proposal.' The programme focuses on conditions necessary for market efficiency although the report is a wider exploration of public interest. Under the section on 'Constraints to Wants', the framework specifically states, 'externalities result in sub-optimal resource allocation because there is no clear economic effect on those using the resources'. This will be useful when considering the public interest statements of all the organizations referred to in this chapter, especially those not based on an international treaty.

53 www.icaew.com/-/media/corporate/files/about-icaew/who-we-are/charters-bye-laws/supplemental-charter-of-the-21st-december-1948.ashx (Accessed 12 August 2025.)

54 Under Schedule 10 and 11 of the 2006 Companies Act.

55 https://media.frc.org.uk/documents/Public_Interest_Criteria.pdf (Accessed 12 August 2025.)

56 www.ifac.org/knowledge-gateway/accountancy-policy/publications/definition-public-interest (Accessed 12 August 2025.)

57 See Chapter 2, Note 41.

58 https://ipiob.org/document/Public-Interest-Framework-2020.pdf?utm (Accessed 12 August 2025.)

59 www.ifrs.org/content/dam/ifrs/about-us/who-we-are/working-in-the-public-interest.pdf (Accessed 12 august 2025.)

60 www.iosco.org/v2/about/?subsection=by-laws (Accessed 12 August 2025.)

61 www.fca.org.uk/news/press-releases/fca-publishes-mission-business-plan-2017-18?utm (Accessed 12 August 2025.)

Conclusion to Part 1

1 Michel Foucault, *Power/Knowledge: Selected Interviews and Other Writings, 1972–1977*. Edited by Colin Gordon. Pantheon Books, 1980, p. 131.

2 www.icas.com/news-insights-events/news/sustainability/peter-bakker-explains-how-accountants-can-save-the-world (Accessed 12 August 2025.)

3 www.wbcsd.org/events/vision-2050-virtual-launch-event-2021/ (Accessed 12 August 2025.)

4 www.icaew.com/insights/insights-specials/when-chartered-accountants-save-the-world/its-time-for-chartered-accountants-to-save-the-world (Accessed 5 February 2025.)

5 www.minterellison.com/-/media/Minter-Ellison/Campaigns/Podcasts/Podcast-Transcript---Barker-and-Joubert.ashx?utm (Accessed 12 August 2025.)

Part 2: How did we come to this?

1 Most histories of accounting start back in Mesopotamia, around 5000 BC, with clerks making lists of what was in the store house and money spent and goods received. This moves on to a history of double-entry book-keeping and the accounting profession and where and when this may have started. Way ahead is Kautilya's Arthasastra (Kautilya, *The Arthashastra*), written in the fourth century BC, which included a system for financial record keeping and audit. But Luca Pacioli, a Franciscan friar, generally gets star billing for double-entry book-keeping. He wrote the snappily titled *Summa de Arithmetica, Geometria, Proportioni et Proportionalità* that included, among other things, a section on

double-entry book-keeping. Benedetto Cotrugli described double-entry in his (slightly earlier book but equally snappy) *Della Mercatura e del Mercante Perfetto* but somehow missed the same level of recognition. Earlier still was Johannes Widmann's *Mercantile Arithmetic,* a German arithmetic book published in 1489 and the first known to use 'plus' and 'minus' signs to represent excess and deficiency in a commercial context. The original title *Behende und hüpsche Rechenung auff allen Kauffmanschafft* or 'Nimble and Neat Calculation for All Mercantile Matters' is the best title but there is a still earlier claim from Amatino Manucci, an Italian merchant based in France. His handwritten financial records from the end of the thirteenth century show the basics of double-entry book-keeping.

2 Cristea, Stefana, Delia David and Luminița Păiușan. 'Specific Features of Islamic Accounting and Cultural Paradigm.' *Munich Personal RePEc Archive*, MPRA Paper no. 27174, 2010, mpra.ub.uni-muenchen.de/27174/1/specific_features_of_islamic_accounting_and_cultural_paradigm.pdf.

3 It would be possible to start earlier. One option might be the Roman Empire and rise of Christianity separating human beings from the rest of life and the doctrines of dominion 'over' created the permission for behaviours that led to the neglect of certain costs within accounting.

Chapter 3: Eleventh to sixteenth century

1 McGlaughlin, Mary and Bonnnie Wheeler. *The Letters of Heloise and Abelard.* 2009.

2 https://wordhistories.net/2021/11/15/hell-good-intentions/?utm (Accessed 27 August 2025.)

3 Qur'an, Az-Zalzalah 99, 7–8.

4 www.parliament.uk/about/living-heritage/evolutionofparliament/parliamentwork/offices-and-ceremonies/overview/lord-chancellor1/?utm (Accessed 4 June 2025.)

5 *Summa Theologica*, by Thomas Aquinas, 1265–1273.

6 Alves, André Azevedo and Inês Gregório. 'Price Controls and Market Economies,' in *Christianity and Market Regulation*. Edited by Daniel

A. Crane and Samuel Gregg. Cambridge University Press, 2021, pp. 213–232.

7 The idea that non-humans might be able to claim redress has to wait a few centuries.

8 ideas.repec.org/p/pra/mprapa/11012.html (Accessed 12 August 2025.)

9 One of the first examples was with the East India Company in 1740 of which more to come.

10 Qur'an 9:60.

11 Or lords of the land.

12 Federici, *Silvia. Caliban and the Witch: Women, the Body and Primitive Accumulation*. Autonomedia, 2004.

13 For example, in the UK www.legislation.gov.uk/uksi/2014/2916/contents/made

14 Ibid. p. 75.

15 Caroline P. Murphy. 'In Praise of the Ladies of Bologna': The Image and Identity of the Sixteenth-Century Bolognese Female Patriciate. *Renaissance Studies*, vol. 13, no. 4, 1999, pp. 440–454.

16 Under civil law, civil codes restricted married women's legal capacities.

17 https://dialnet.unirioja.es/servlet/articulo?codigo=9228519 (Accessed 12 August 2025.)

18 https://cdn.nationalarchives.gov.uk/documents/research/women-in-chancery.pdf (Accessed 12 August 2025.)

19 See Chapter 3, Note 14.

20 Miley, Frances Myfanwy and Andrew Farley Read. 'Accounting Lessons from a Medieval Woman: The Writing of Christine de Pisan.' European Accounting Association 39th Annual Congress, Maastricht, the Netherlands, May 2016.

21 Hoskin, Keith and Richard Macve. 'Writing, Examining, Disciplining: The Genesis of Accounting's Modern Power' in *Accounting as Social and Institutional Practice*. Edited by Anthony G. Hopwood and Peter Miller, Cambridge University Press, 1994, pp. 67–97.

22 'Medieval Women with Eleanor Janega.' Gone Medieval, hosted by Cat Jarman, History Hit, 7 March 2023, access.historyhit.com/videos/medieval-women-janega

Chapter 4: Seventeenth to eighteenth century

1 Through the Treaty of Tordesillas (1494) (Treaty of Tordesillas | Summary, Definition, Map, & Facts | Britannica) following the Papal Bull 'Inter Caetera' (1493) (Inter Caetera – Papal Encyclicals).

2 https://encyclopediavirginia.org/entries/smythe-sir-thomas-ca-1558-1625/?utm (Accessed 12 August 2025.)

3 www.cambridge.org/core/journals/european-journal-of-sociology-archives-europeennes-de-sociologie/article/empires-famine-and-the-significance-of-the-political-economy-of-colonialism-from-the-mughal-empire-to-british-colonial-rule-in-india/8412E24F05772E53C6149D92570B5A6F?utm (Accessed 12 August 2025.)

4 https://insights.aib.world/article/90323-_imagine-a-better-world_-an-interview-with-paul-polman-aib-2023-international-executive-of-the-year? (Accessed 12 August 2025.)

5 *Moses v Macferlan* (1760) referred to an obligation based on natural justice and equity.

6 https://existentialtheology.com/99-against-the-slavery-of-christians-creator-omnium?utm (Accessed 12 August 2025.)

7 Hanke, Lewis. 'Pope Paul III and the American Indians.' *Harvard Theological Review*, vol. 30, no. 2, April 1937, p. 77.

8 https://international-review.icrc.org/sites/default/files/S0020860400070960a.pdf (Accessed 12 August 2025.)

9 Brown, Christopher Leslie. *Moral Capital: Foundations of British Abolitionism*. University of North Carolina Press, 2006.

10 The Bible, Leviticus 24:44.

11 www.cambridge.org/core/journals/journal-of-global-history/article/on-the-economic-importance-of-the-slave-plantation-complex-to-the-british-economy-during-the-eighteenth-century-a-valueadded-approach/DBB1225FF928C09689B3EEFCA8F66C55 (Accessed 12 August 2025.)

[12] www.theatlantic.com/business/archive/2014/12/empire-of-cotton/383660/ (Accessed March 2025.)

[13] Saini, Angela. *The Patriarchs: The Origins of Inequality*. HarperCollins, 2023, p. 165.

[14] www.vox.com/identities/2019/8/16/20806069/slavery-economy-capitalism-violence-cotton-edward-baptist (Accessed March 2025.)

[15] Akala. *Natives: Race and Class in the Ruins of Empire*. John Murray, 2018, Chapter 2.

[16] Williams, Gomer. *History of the Liverpool Privateers and Letters of Marque with an Account of the Liverpool Slave Trade*. Originally published 1897. W. Heineman, p. 596.

[17] Darity, W. A. and A. K. Mullen. *From Here to Equality: Reparations for Black Americans in the Twenty-First Century*. University of North Carolina Press, 2020.

[18] www.who.int/news-room/fact-sheets/detail/obesity-and-overweight (Accessed 12 August 2025.)

[19] www.bmj.com/content/346/bmj.e7492 (Accessed 12 August 2025.)

[20] https://council.science/blog/the-environmental-impact-of-cotton-production/?utm (Accessed 12 August 2025.)

[21] In the United States, Native American reservations cover 56 million acres, United States, Department of the Interior, Bureau of Indian Affairs. 'What Is a Federal Indian Reservation?' *Bureau of Indian Affairs*, 19 August 2017, www.bia.gov/faqs/what-federal-indian-reservation (Accessed 12 August 2025.)

[22] https://teara.govt.nz/en/te-tai/about-treaty-settlements? (Accessed 12 August 2025.)

[23] www.msd.govt.nz/about-msd-and-our-work/publications-resources/statistics/covid-19/who-received-the-covid-19-wage-subsidies-may-2022.html?utm (Accessed 12 August 2025.)

[24] Rublack, Ulinka and Maria Hayward, editors. *The First Book of Fashion: The Book of Clothes of Matthäus & Veit Konrad Schwarz of Augsburg*. Bloomsbury, 2015.

[25] Steinmetz, Gred. *The Richest Man Who Ever Lived: The Life and Times of Jacob Fugger*. Simon and Shuster, 2015.

[26] Baladouni, Vahe. 'Financial Reporting in the Early Years of the East India Company.' *Accounting Historians Journal*, vol. 13, no. 1, Spring 1986, article 3, pp. 1–26. https://egrove.olemiss.edu/aah_journal/vol13/iss1/3/

[27] Mair, John. *Book-keeping Methodiz'd: Or, a Methodical Treatise of Merchant-Accompts, According to the Italian Form*. 2nd edn, with additions and improvements, London, 1741. *Internet Archive*, https://archive.org/details/bookkeepingmetho00mair (Accessed 24 September 2025.)

[28] Rosenthal, Caitlin. *Accounting for Slavery: Masters and Management*. Harvard University Press, 2018.

[29] Risk materializing and how this relates to materiality will be important later.

Chapter 5: Nineteenth century to 1973

[1] https://reparationscomm.org/reparations-news/britains-colonial-shame-slave-owners-given-huge-payouts-after-abolition/? (Accessed 12 August 2025.)

[2] www.theguardian.com/news/2018/mar/29/slavery-abolition-compensation-when-will-britain-face-up-to-its-crimes-against-humanity?utm (Accessed 13 October 2025.)

[3] https://cornerofgenealogy.com/sugar-boom-and-bust/ (Accessed 12 August 2025.)

[4] Smith, Adam. *An Inquiry into the Nature and Causes of the Wealth of Nations*. Edited by Edwin Cannan, Modern Library, 1994.

[5] Rogers, Meeghan, Gareth Campbell, and John Turner. 'From Complementary to Competitive: The London and U.K. Provincial Stock Markets.' *The Journal of Economic History*, vol. 80, no. 2, June 2020, pp. 501–530. Cambridge University Press.

[6] Try suggesting that a sustainable future is one without usury and see what happens now.

7 Or a remedy to use the language of the UN Guiding Principles on Business and Human Rights.

8 The recent interest in purpose led business is something of a return to having an objects clause, though without the potential liability of directors for acting outside of those objects.

9 https://articles.obr.uk/300-years-of-uk-public-finance-data/index.html? (Accessed 24 September 2025.)

10 Raised again passing during COVID.

11 Loft, Anne. 'Accountancy and the First World War.' *Accounting as Social and Institutional Practice*. Edited by Anthony G. Hopwood and Peter Miller, Cambridge Studies in Management, Cambridge University Press, 1994, pp. 273–301.

12 https://www.imf.org/en/Blogs/Articles/2019/01/02/new-data-on-global-debt?utm (Accessed 8 October 2025.)

13 www.oecd.org/en/publications/global-debt-report-2025_8ee42b13-en.html?utm (Accessed 12 August 2025.)

14 www.weforum.org/stories/2024/10/imf-global-debt-and-other-economy-stories-21-october/?utm (Accessed 12 August 2025.)

15 www.imf.org/external/datamapper/GDD/2024%20Global%20Debt%20Monitor.pdf?utm (Accessed 12 August 2025.)

16 https://president.az/en/articles/view/67324 (Accessed 12 August 2025.)

17 Somewhere along the line even their machine agents operate to code written by people.

18 It's not true https://scienceinfo.net/the-truth-about-the-story-of-boiled-frog.html (accessed 24 September 2025) – though it would appear to be true for human beings.

19 https://archive.gyford.com/2009/04/28/www.geocities.com/Paris/LeftBank/1914/fumifug.html (Accessed 12 August 2025.)

20 Zola, Émile. *Germinal*. Translated by Leonard Tancock, Penguin Classics, 1954.

21 www.iea.org/reports/coal-in-the-energy-supply-of-china (Accessed 12 August 2025.)

22 www.iea.org/data-and-statistics/charts/world-oil-supply-and-demand-1971-2020 (Accessed 12 August 2025.)

23 www.theguardian.com/environment/2025/mar/05/half-of-worlds-co2-emissions-come-from-36-fossil-fuel-firms-study-shows?utm (Accessed 12 August 2025.)

24 https://victorianweb.org/economics/ridley3.html (Accessed 12 August 2025.)

25 In comedy this would be an example of a call back to an earlier discussion of the same idea. There are a lot of these to watch for.

26 www.icaew.com/-/media/corporate/files/about-icaew/who-we-are/charters-bye-laws/supplemental-charter-of-the-21st-december-1948.ashx (Accessed 12 August 2025.)

27 Chandler, Roy and Dick Edwards. Creating Accountability, *Accountancy*, April 2000.

28 https://commons.lib.jmu.edu/cgi/viewcontent.cgi?article=1285&context=honors201019&utm (Accessed 12 August 2025.)

Chapter 6: 1973 to now

1 You, Leyuan, et al. 'An Empirical Study of Multiple Direct International Listings.' *Global Finance Journal*, vol. 24, no. 1, 2013, pp. 69–84.

2 https://data.worldbank.org/indicator/CM.MKT.LCAP.CD?end=2020&most_recent_value_desc=true&start=1975 (Accessed 30 May 2025.)

3 Asset managers charge a fee based on the amount of assets they are managing on behalf of other investors.

4 Maher, Stephen and Scott M. Aquanno. *The Fall and Rise of American Finance: From J.P. Morgan to BlackRock*. Verso, 13 February 2024.

5 Ruggie, John. Protect, Respect and Remedy: A Framework for Business and Human Rights. Report of the Special Representative of the Secretary-General on the Issue of Human Rights and Transnational Corporations and Other Business Enterprises, United Nations Human

Rights Council, 7 April 2008, A/HRC/8/5. https://media.business-humanrights.org/media/documents/files/reports-and-materials/Ruggie-report-7-Apr-2008.pdf Page 189 (Accessed 12 August 2025.)

6 Ibid.

7 https://reports.weforum.org/docs/WEF_GGGR_2025.pdf (Accessed 28 August 2025.)

8 www.unwomen.org/sites/default/files/2025-03/adolescent-girls-rights-over-30-years-en.pdf Page 35 (Accessed 12 August 2025.)

9 www.who.int/news-room/fact-sheets/detail/violence-against-women#:~:text=A%202018%20analysis%20of%20prevalence%20data%20from%202000%E2%80%932018,physical%20and%2For%20sexual%20violence%20by%20an%20intimate%20 (Accessed 12 August 2025.)

10 See Chapter 2, Note 56.

11 Jones, Phil. *Work Without the Worker: Labour in the Age of Platform Capitalism*. Verso, 2021.

12 Ibid.

13 www.globaljustice.org.uk/resource/honest-accounts-2017-how-world-profits-africas-wealth/ (Accessed 12 August 2025.)

14 Impact can too easily be means of claiming positive impacts and ignoring negative impacts irrespective of causality.

15 https://wcms_575479.pdf (Accessed March 2025.)

16 www.theguardian.com/world/2025/feb/25/beatings-torture-and-electric-shocks-freed-scam-compound-workers-allege-horrific-abuse?utm (Accessed 12 August 2025.)

17 United Nations. *The Sustainable Development Goals Report 2023: Special Edition*. United Nations, 2023. https://unstats.un.org/sdgs/report/2023/

18 https://globalchallenges.ch/issue/6/land-grabs-big-business-and-large-scale-damages/?utm (Accessed 12 August 2025.)

19 https://iwgia.org/images/publications/new-publications/land-grabbing-indigenous-peoples-rights.compressed.pdf?utm (Accessed 12 August 2025.)

[20] https://grain.org/article/entries/4479-grain-releases-data-set-with-over-400-global-land-grabs (Accessed 12 August 2025.)

[21] https://wealthofthecommons.org/essay/feminism-and-politics-commons/ (Accessed 22 April 2025.)

[22] First explored by Garrett Hardin in 1968, who argued that there was an inherent conflict between individual self-interest and the common good within shared resources. Hardin, Garrett. 'The Tragedy of the Commons.' *Science*, vol. 162, no. 3859, 1968, pp. 1243–1248.

[23] www.usda.gov/about-usda/general-information/initiatives-and-highlighted-programs/peoples-garden/importance-pollinators?utm (Accessed 12 August 2025.)

[24] 'Pollinator Deficits, Food Consumption, and Consequences for Human Health: A Modeling Study.' *Environmental Health Perspectives*, vol. 130, no. 12. ehp.niehs.nih.gov/doi/10.1289/EHP10947

[25] https://beeculture.com/2022-almond-pollination-outlook/?utm (Accessed 12 August 2025.)

[26] Worldwide decline of the entomofauna: A review of its drivers. www.sciencedirect.com/science/article/abs/pii/S0006320718313636

[27] https://openknowledge.fao.org/server/api/core/bitstreams/66538eba-9c85-4504-8438-c1cf0a0a3903/content/sofia/2024/status-of-fishery-resources.html (Accessed 12 August 2025.)

[28] https://ourworldindata.org/palm-oil?utm (Accessed 12 August 2025.)

[29] www.theguardian.com/environment/2025/mar/10/microplastics-hinder-plant-photosynthesis-study-finds-threatening-millions-with-starvation?CMP=Share_iOSApp_Other (Accessed 12 August 2025.)

[30] www.theguardian.com/environment/2025/aug/03/world-in-15tn-plastics-crisis-hitting-health-from-infancy-to-old-age-report-warns?CMP=Share_iOSApp_Other (Accessed 5 August 2025.)

[31] Hickel, Jason, et al. 'A Fair-Shares Assessment of Resource Use, 1970–2017.' *The Lancet Planetary Health*, vol. 6, no. 7, 2022, pp. e586–e596. ScienceDirect, https://doi.org/10.1016/S2542-5196(22)00044-4 (Accessed 24 September 2025.)

[32] www.unep.org/news-and-stories/story/were-gobbling-earths-resources-unsustainable-rate?utm (Accessed 6 August 2025.)

33 https://doi.org/10.1016/S2542-5196(22)00044-4hive.greenfinanceinstitute.com/wp-content/uploads/2024/04/GFI-GREENING-FINANCE-FOR-NATURE-FINAL-FULL-REPORT-RDS4.pdf (Accessed 12 August 2025.)

34 www.corteidh.or.cr/docs/opiniones/seriea_32_en.pdf?utm (Accessed 28 August 2025.)

35 International Court of Justice. *Obligations of States in Respect of Climate Change: Advisory Opinion*. 23 July 2025. International Court of Justice, www.icj-cij.org/case/187 (Accessed 7 October 2025.)

Chapter 7: Financial accounting, 1973 to date

1 Kirsch, Robert J. *The International Accounting Standards Committee: A Political History*. Wolters Kluwer (UK) Limited, 2006, p. 20.

2 Where I trained, before it became PwC.

3 www.financestrategists.com/accounting/introduction-to-accounting/international-accounting-standards-committee-iasc/ (Accessed 12 August 2025.)

4 Ibid.

5 American Institute of Certified Public Accountants. Objectives of Financial Statements: Report of the Study Group. Chaired by Robert M. Trueblood, AICPA, 1973.

6 Ibid.

7 Op. cit.

8 Op. cit.

9 Op. cit.

10 Op. cit.

11 Young, Joni J. 'Making Up Users.' *Accounting, Organizations and Society*, vol. 31, no. 6, 2006, pp. 579–600. And also for a more complete and detailed analysis of the history running up to these conclusions.

12 See Chapter 7, Note 5.

13 See Chapter 7, Note 5.

14 International Accounting Standards Board. *Conceptual Framework for Financial Reporting*. IFRS Foundation, March 2018.

15 International Accounting Standards Committee. Framework for the Preparation and Presentation of Financial Statements. IASC, 1989.

16 Tweedie, David, Allan Cook, and Geoffrey Whittington. *The UK Accounting Standards Board, 1990–2000: Restoring Honesty and Trust in Accounting*. Routledge, 2024.

17 www.icaew.com/library/research-guides/international-accounting-standards?utm (Accessed 12 August 2025.)

18 'Minutes of the 10 December 2008, Conceptual Framework (Phase A & Phase D) Board Meeting.' *Financial Accounting Standards Board*, 10 December 2008.

19 'The Primary User Group, Entity Perspective and Parent Company Approach.' *International Accounting Standards Board*, March 2009, www.ifrs.org/content/dam/ifrs/meetings/2009/march/joint-iasb-efrag/conceptual-framework/ap3b-the-primary-user-group-entity-perspective-and-parent-company-approach.pdf (Accessed 12 August 2025.)

20 Entity is the language used in the IFRS Conceptual Framework for an organization that is most commonly a business.

21 www.ifrs.org/content/dam/ifrs/project/conceptual-framework-2010/conceptual-framework-exposure-draft.pdf?utm (Accessed 12 August 2025.)

22 International Public Sector Accounting Standards Board. 2025 Handbook of International Public Sector Accounting Pronouncements. International Federation of Accountants, 2025.) The Conceptual Framework for General Purpose financial Reporting by Public entities, Chapter 2.

23 See Note 21 above.

24 Jackson, Tim. 'The False Economy of Big Food and the Case for a New Food Economy.' *Food, Farming and Countryside Commission*, 2024.

25 www.gov.uk/government/statistics/corporation-tax-statistics-2024/corporation-tax-statistics-commentary-2024 (Accessed 12 August 2025.)

26 Ibid.

27 www.theguardian.com/business/2023/aug/22/pwc-partners-to-be-paid-906000-this-year (Accessed 12 August 2025.)

28 Kees Camfferman. International Accounting Standard Setting and Geopolitics. *Accounting in Europe*, vol. 17, no. 3, 2020, pp. 243–263, DOI: 10.1080/17449480.2020.179521

29 The MOU between the Monitoring Board and IFRS in 2023 includes ISSB and makes 17 references to sustainability, including seven to sustainability disclosures and none to sustainability related financial disclosures as an example of the risk of conflating the two, www.ifrs.org/content/dam/ifrs/groups/monitoring-board/mb-ifrs-mou-2023.pdf (Accessed 12 August 2025.)

30 International Integrated Reporting Council. International <IR> Framework. January 2021, integratedreporting.org/wp-content/uploads/2021/01/InternationalIntegratedReportingFramework.pdf (Accessed 12 August 2025.)

31 Black, Liam and Nicholls, Jeremy. *There's No Business Like Social Business: How to Be Socially Enterprising.* The Cat's Pyjamas, 2004.

32 https://doughnuteconomics.org/tools/doughnut-design-for-business-core-tool (Accessed 12 August 2025.)

33 https://finance.ec.europa.eu/capital-markets-union-and-financial-markets/company-reporting-and-auditing/company-reporting/corporate-sustainability-reporting_en (Accessed 12 August 2025.)

34 www.consilium.europa.eu/en/press/press-releases/2023/12/14/corporate-sustainability-due-diligence-council-and-parliament-strike-deal-to-protect-environment-and-human-rights/ (Accessed 12 August 2025.)

35 For example, www.thelandbankinggroup.com (Accessed 12 August 2025.)

36 https://capitalscoalition.org/project/nature-on-the-balance-sheet/ (Accessed 12 August 2025.)

37 COP stands for Conference of the Parties which is UNFCCC governing body.

38 COP 30 is in November 2025.

39 www.bbc.co.uk/news/articles/cd7575x8yq5o (Accessed 29 May 2025.)

40 https://unstats.un.org/sdgs/report/2023/Goal-05/?utm (Accessed 25 August 2025.)

41 www.icaew.com/library/research-guides/uk-auditing-standards? (Accessed 12 August 2025.)

42 https://seea.un.org/ (Accessed 12 August 2025.)

43 https://unstats.un.org/unsd/nationalaccount/sna.asp (Accessed 3 February 2025.)

44 www.consilium.europa.eu/media/64307/g7-communique-20230513.pdf (Accessed 12 August 2025.)

45 www.gov.wales/well-being-future-generations-act-essentials-html (Accessed 12 August 2025.)

46 www.audit.wales/about-us (Accessed 12 August 2025.)

47 www.audit.wales/sites/default/files/Well-being-of-Future-Generations-report-eng_11.pdf (Accessed 12 August 2025

48 www.treasury.govt.nz/publications/well-being-budget/well-being-budget-2023-support-today-building-tomorrow?utm (Accessed 23 April 2025.)

49 https://treasury.gov.au/policy-topics/measuring-what-matters (Accessed 12 August 2025.)

50 www.oecd.org/en/topics/measuring-well-being-and-progress.html (Accessed 23 April 2025.)

51 See Chapter 7, Note 49.

52 www.iso.org/standard/65038.html (Accessed 23 April 2025.)

53 PAS 808:2022. Purpose-Driven Organizations – Worldviews, Principles and Behaviours for Sustainable Performance. British Standards Institution, 2022.

54 www.bsigroup.com/en-GB/insights-and-media/insights/brochures/pas-808-purpose-driven-organizations-for-delivering-sustainability/ (Accessed 12 August 2025.)

55 Jackson, Tim. *Prosperity Without Growth: Foundations for the Economy of Tomorrow*. 2nd edn, Routledge, 2017.

56 www.thelancet.com/journals/lanplh/article/PIIS2542-5196(24)00310-3/fulltext?mcp (Accessed 12 August 2025.)

57 www.iso.org/standard/86672.html (Accessed 12 August 2025.)

58 www.socialvalueint.org/standards-and-guidance (Accessed 14 August 2025.)

59 https://capitalscoalition.org/capitals-approach/ (Accessed 12 August 2025.)

60 https://capitalscoalition.org/capitals-approach/frameworkintegrated/ (Accessed 12 August 2025.)

Conclusion to Part 2

1 www.actionagainsthunger.org/the-hunger-crisis/world-hunger-facts/?utm (Accessed 6 June 2025.)

2 www.oxfam.org/en/press-releases/just-8-men-own-same-wealth-half-world (Accessed 12 August 2025.)

3 Stiglitz, Joseph E. 'The New Era of Monopoly Is Here.' *The Guardian*, 13 May 2016, www.theguardian.com/business/2016/may/13/-new-era-monopoly-joseph-stiglitz

4 https://ips-dc.org/report-americas-wealth-dynasties-2021/ (Accessed 24 September 2025.)

5 OECD (2008), The Polluter Pays Principle: Definition, Analysis, Implementation, OECD Publishing, Paris, https://doi.org/10.1787/9789264044845-en.

6 www.theguardian.com/environment/2025/jun/19/uk-toxic-air-killing-people-doctors-warn?CMP=Share_iOSApp_Other (Accessed 14 August 2025.)

7 www.stateofglobalair.org/resources/report/state-global-air-report-2024?utm (Accessed 14 August 2025.)

8 https://us.boell.org/en/unpacking-finance-loss-and-damage (Accessed 24 April 2025.)

9 www.reuters.com/legal/judge-says-social-media-companies-must-face-lawsuits-over-harm-children-2023-11-14/?utm (Accessed 14 April 2025.)

10 Facebook. Teen Mental Health Deep Dive. 2019. FBarchive, edited by Latanya Sweeney, Public Interest Tech Lab, 2023, https://fbarchive.org (Accessed 14 April 2025.)

11 https://businesstelegraph.co.uk/misogynistic-content-driving-uk-boys-to-hunt-vulnerable-girls-on-suicide-forums/ (Accessed 22 April 2025.)

12 www.wsj.com/articles/korea-zinc-backs-trump-plan-for-deep-sea-mining-f4b9a3fc?utm (Accessed 14 August 2025.)

13 www.bbc.co.uk/news/articles/cq69e4j6jz8o (Accessed 12 August 2025.)

14 www.mckinsey.com/global-themes/digital-disruption/harnessing-automation-for-a-future-that-works (Accessed 15 April 2025.)

15 www.mckinsey.com/capabilities/mckinsey-digital/our-insights/the-economic-potential-of-generative-ai-the-next-productivity-frontier?utm (Accessed 15 April 2025.)

16 www.un.org/en/about-us/universal-declaration-of-human-rights (Accessed 23 April 2025.)

Part 3: What can we do?

1 The possibility is referenced in Paragraph 1.11 of the IFRS Conceptual Framework

2 www.marxists.org/archive/marx/works/1845/theses/theses.htm?utm_source (Accessed 28 August 2025.)

Chapter 8: A new purpose and a glimmer of hope

1 Included in paragraph 4 of the 2030 Agenda for Sustainable Development and in subsequent guidance unsdg.un.org/2030-agenda/universal-values/leave-no-one-behind?utm (Accessed 24 April 2025.)

2 The principle of Do no Harm is included in UNDP Human Rights Based Approach toolkit, the UNDP Risk Appetite Statement and the UNDP Global Programme on the Rule of Law and Human Rights.

[3] International Accounting Standards Board. Conceptual Framework for Financial Reporting. IFRS Foundation, March 2018.

[4] Ibid.

[5] FASB also has a Conceptual Framework which follows the same logic in para OB3. Financial Accounting Standards Board. *Conceptual Framework for Financial Reporting*. September 2024.

[6] Remember the Report of the Study Group on the Objectives of Financial Statements.

[7] Christov-Moore, Leonardo, and Marco Iacoboni. 'Sex Differences in Somatomotor Representations of Others' Pain: A Permutation-Based Analysis.' Brain Structure and Function, vol. 224, no. 2, Mar. 2019, pp. 937–947. Springer. https://doi.org/10.1007/s00429-018-1814-y

[8] https://newsroom.ucla.edu/stories/womens-brains-show-more-empathy (Accessed 14 August 2025.)

[9] Saini, Angela. *The Patriarchs: The Origins of Inequality*. HarperCollins, 2023, p. 183.

[10] https://www.theguardian.com/us-news/ng-interactive/2025/apr/08/empathy-sin-christian-right-musk-trump?utm (Accessed 14 August 2025.)

[11] Echean, Veeranud. *Aligning Values with Returns: Ethical Investing in Personal Finance*. Preprint, May 2024. ResearchGate, doi:10.13140/RG.2.2.13087.16802/2

[12] Bachmann, Kremena, Julia Meyer and Annette Krauss. 'Investment Motives and Performance Expectations of Impact Investors.' *Journal of Behavioral and Experimental Finance*, vol. 42, 2024, article 100911. doi:org/10.1016/j.jbef.2024.100911

[13] Bauer, Rob, Tobias Ruof and Paul Smeets. 'Get Real! Individuals Prefer More Sustainable Investments.' *The Review of Financial Studies*, vol. 34, no. 8, August 2021, pp. 3976–4043. doi.org/10.1093/rfs/hhab031

[14] www.fundecomarket.co.uk/help/financial-lives-survey-2024-responsible-investment-highlights/ (Accessed 6 August 2025.)

[15] moneywise.com/research/ethical-investing (Accessed 14 August 2025.)

[16] Smith, Adam. *The Theory of Moral Sentiments*. Edited by Knud Haakonssen, Cambridge University Press, 2002. And many thanks to Elena Douglas for introducing me to this.

[17] www.weforum.org/stories/2023/04/ranked-the-largest-bond-markets-in-the-world/?utm (Accessed 14 August 2025.)

[18] Estimated from www.imf.org/en/Blogs/Articles/2021/12/15/blog-global-debt-reaches-a-record-226-trillion (Accessed 14 August 2025.)

[19] International Public Sector Accounting Standards Board. The Conceptual Framework for General Purpose Financial Reporting by Public Sector Entities. International Federation of Accountants (IFAC), October 2014.

[20] Ibid.

[21] Op. cit.

[22] HM Treasury. The Green Book: Central Government Guidance on Appraisal and Evaluation. 2022 ed., HM Treasury, 2022.

[23] For example, Section 2.2 states, 'Appraisal is the process of assessing the costs, benefits and risks of alternative ways to meet government objectives. It helps decision makers to understand the potential effects, trade-offs and overall impact of options by providing an objective evidence base for decision making.' In Section 2.3, the Green Book also makes it clear that social value includes all significant costs and benefits that affect well-being of the population. 'The appraisal of social value, also known as public value, is based on the principles and ideas of welfare economics and concerns overall social welfare efficiency, not simply economic market efficiency. Social or public value therefore includes all significant costs and benefits that affect the welfare and well-being of the population, not just market effects. For example, environmental, cultural, health, social care, justice and security effects are included. This welfare and well-being consideration applies to the entire population that is served by the government, not simply taxpayers' (Section 2.3).

[24] www.ipsasb.org/publications/recommended-practice-guideline-3-1 (Accessed 14 August 2025.)

[25] Some jurisdictions do require similar information. For example, New Zealand has PBE FRS 48 Service Performance Reporting which requires non-financial information on performance against service objectives.

26 www.ifac.org/_flysystem/azure-private/meetings/files/7-Reporting-Sustainability-Program-Info_Final.pdf

27 www.xrb.govt.nz/sustainability-reporting/he-tauira-an-overview/ (Accessed 14 August 2025.)

28 Table 4.2 in the IFRS Conceptual Framework.

29 European Union. *Directive 2013/34/EU of the European Parliament and of the Council of 26 June 2013 on the annual financial statements, consolidated financial statements and related reports of certain types of undertakings.* Official Journal of the European Union, L 182, 29 June 2013, pp. 19–76. EUR-Lex, Paragraph 9.

30 Imagen Fiel is the translation of True and Fair used in the EC Directive – literal translation – 'faithful image'.

31 España. Real Decreto de 22 de agosto de 1885 por el que se publica el Código de Comercio. Boletín Oficial del Estado, 1885. www.boe.es/buscar/doc.php?id=BOE-A-1885-6627

32 Spain. Real Decreto Legislativo 1/2010, de 2 de julio, por el que se aprueba el texto refundido de la Ley de Sociedades de Capital. Boletín Oficial del Estado, no. 161, 3 July 2010, pp. 58486–58655. www.boe.es/boe/dias/2010/07/03/pdfs/BOE-A-2010-10544.pdf (Accessed 14 August 2025.)

33 www.mca.gov.in/Ministry/pdf/CompaniesAct2013.pdf (Accessed 24 April 2025.)

34 https://github.com/kaunto/companies-act-2016/blob/master/part-3-management-of-company/division-3-accounts-and-audit/subdivision-1-financial-statements-and-reports/section-249.-general-requirements-for-financial-statements.md (Accessed 25 September 2025.)

35 www5.austlii.edu.au/au/legis/cth/consol_act/ca2001172/s297.html (Accessed 14 August 2025.)

36 https://ojk.go.id/en/regulasi/Documents/Pages/Guidelines-for-Preparing-Comfort-Letters/12.%20VIIIG7.pdf?utm (Accessed 14 August 2025.)

37 www.frc.org.uk/library/standards-codes-policy/accounting-and-reporting/true-and-fair-concept/ (Accessed 14 August 2025.)

[38] Ibid.

[39] www.kering.com/api/download-file/?path=KERING_2023_URD_EN_01eada3a94.pdf Page 222 (Accessed 1 August 2025.)

[40] https://ddd.uab.cat/pub/infanu/239915/iaKERINGa2023ieng.pdf Page 6 (Accessed 1 August 2025.)

[41] Felix Midco Ltd is the parent company for TrustedHouseSitters Ltd, a house and pet sitting platform.

[42] Accessed from Companies House for Felix Midco, 5 August 2025.

[43] https://static1.squarespace.com/static/60dc51e3c58aef413ae5c975/t/65aee53e9a5b0866faf4c711/1705960801670/True+and+Fair%2C+signed+opinion (Accessed 14 August 2025.)

[44] These have been emphasised in the IFRS Foundation's 'Educational Material', www.ifrs.org/content/dam/ifrs/supporting-implementation/documents/effects-of-climate-related-matters-on-financial-statements.pdf (Accessed 14 August 2025.)

[45] www.socialvalueint.org/s/Are-Your-Financial-Statements-True-and-Fair-UK-company-guide-nnwc.pdf (Accessed 14 August 2025.)

[46] www.socialvalueint.org/s/Reflejan-tus-cuentas-la-imagen-fiel-de-tu-empresa_.pdf (Accessed 14 August 2025.)

[47] https://register-of-charities.charitycommission.gov.uk/en/charity-search/-/charity-details/5020014/accounts-and-annual-returns?utm (Accessed 5 August 2025.)

[48] https://corporate.cyrilamarchandblogs.com/2023/01/how-true-is-true-and-fair-view/ (Accessed 14 August 2025.)

[49] https://tnfd.global/knowledge-hub/example-tnfd-reporting/ (Accessed 14 August 2025.)

[50] Forico Pty Ltd. *Illustrative Example of Integrated TNFD-TCFD Disclosures: FY22.* Taskforce on Nature-related Financial Disclosures, September 2023. https://tnfd.global/wp-content/uploads/2023/09/Forico_Illustrative_Example_of_Integrated_TNFD_TCFD-Disclosures_FY22.pdf (Accessed 14 August 2025.)

[51] Directors' Duties Navigator (Fourth edition, 2024) – CCLI- https://commonwealthclimatelaw.org/directors-duties-navigator-climate-risk-and-sustainability-disclosures-fourth-edition-2024/ (Accessed 25 September 2025.)

[52] Regierungskommission Deutscher Corporate Governance Kodex. *German Corporate Governance Code*. 28 April 2022 starting with the Foreword.

[53] www.hugheshubbard.com/news/consequences-of-the-french-pacte-act-action-plan-for-growth-and-transformation-of-compan ies-on-the-corporate-governance-management-of-companies-based-on-their-interests-and-potentially-their-raison-detre-1 (Accessed 15 April 2025.)

[54] www.thebritishacademy.ac.uk/programmes/future-of-the-corporation/ (Accessed 15 April 2025.)

[55] https://sifocc.org/sifocc_documents/report-on-the-5th-full-sifocc-meet ing/ (Accessed 15 April 2025.)

[56] https://chapterzero.org.uk/climate-law/climate-governance-legislation-and-litigation/uk-legal-opinion-nature-related-risks-and-directors-dut ies/ (Accessed 5 August 2025.)

[57] Commonwealthclimatelaw.org/wp-content/uploads/2023/05/CCLI-Biodiversity-Risk-Legal-Implications-for-Companies-and-their-Directors-December-2022-corrected-May-2023.pdf (Accessed 31 August 2025.)

[58] www.cambridge.org/core/books/abs/tort-law/reasonable-person/19FA3 45C7D50A61EBAB5289568A89ECB (Accessed 14 April 2025.)

[59] www.centerforenvironmentalrights.org/rights-of-nature-law-libr ary?utm (Accessed 14 August 2025.)

[60] www.climatechangenews.com/2025/05/28/peruvian-farmer-loses-clim ate-case-against-rwe-but-paves-way-for-future-action/?utm (Accessed 9 June 2025.)

[61] www.lse.ac.uk/granthaminstitute/publication/global-trends-in-climate-change-litigation-2025-snapshot/ (Accessed 5 August 2025.)

[62] www.iaasb.org/publications/isa-540-revised-auditing-accounting-estima tes-and-related-disclosures-9 (Accessed 14 August 2025.)

[63] www.iaasb.org/publications/isa-315-revised-2019-identifying-and-assess ing-risks-material-misstatement (Accessed 14 August 2025.)

[64] Remembering that managers include directors in the Conceptual Framework.

[65] Conceptual Framework paragraph 1.4.

[66] See Chapter 3, Note 52.

[67] www.gov.uk/guidance/public-benefit-rules-for-charities (Accessed 28 August 2025.)

[68] www.egora.fr/actus-pro/remuneration/trop-rentable-la-biologie-la-profession-appelle-ne-pas-sacrifier-le-secteur?utm (Accessed 12 August 2025.)

[69] https://docs.un.org/en/A/CONF.227/2025/L.1 para 34 (b) (Accessed 6 August 2025.)

[70] Hurth, Victoria, Ben Renshaw and Lorenzo Fioramonti. *Beyond Profit: Purpose-Driven Leadership for a Well-being Economy*. John Murray Business, 2025.

[71] www.iso.org/standard/86112.html (Accessed 12 August 2025.)

[72] https://sdgprivatefinance.undp.org/resources/publications (Accessed 12 August 2025.)

[73] www.socialvalueint.org/sdg-assurance-scheme#case-study (Accessed 28 August 2025.)

Chapter 9: Changing accounting and auditing

[1] See Chapter 7, Note 13.

[2] accounting-streams.org/principles-of-accounting/12.html (Accessed 17 August 2025.)

[3] Flèche, Sarah, and Cyrille Schwellnus. Valuing Business Impacts in the Areas of Wage Inequality and Employee Well-Being. OECD Publishing, 2023, www.oecd.org/content/dam/oecd/en/publications/reports/2023/06/valuing-business-impacts-in-the-areas-of-wage-inequality-and-employee-well-being_5477adfc/740deb2f-en.pdf (Accessed 14 August 2025.)

[4] Sedilekova, Z., J. Ramos, M. Graham, L. Luyt. Corporate Governance for Nature. In: *The Palgrave Handbook of Environmental Policy and Law*. Palgrave Studies in Sustainable Futures. Palgrave Macmillan, Cham, 2025. https://doi.org/10.1007/978-3-031-30231-2_17-1 (Accessed 24 September 2025.)

5 IFRS Foundation. IFRS 13 Fair Value Measurement. IFRS Foundation, 2011.

6 www.impactvaluationhub.org/ (Accessed 14 August 2025.)

7 https://capitalscoalition.org/project/value-accounting-network/ (Accessed 14 August 2025.)

8 https://capitalscoalition.org/project/the-value-commission/ (Accessed 14 August 2025.)

9 www.gistimpact.com/ (Accessed 14 August 2025.)

10 www.simetrica-jacobs.com/ (Accessed 14 August 2025.)

11 www.valuingimpact.com/ (Accessed 14 August 2025.)

12 www.esvd.net/ (Accessed 14 August 2025.)

13 Capitals Coalition. *Accounting for Value: Emerging Approaches of Integrated Profit & Loss and Impact Statements.* Capitals Coalition, 2025. https://capitalscoalition.org/publication/accounting-for-value-emerging-approaches-of-integrated-profit-loss-and-impact-statements/ (Accessed 12 August 2025.)

14 https://masb.org.my/pdf.php?pdf=Accounting%20for%20Zakat%20TRi-1.pdf&file_path=uploadfile (Accessed 6 August 2025.)

15 See Chapter 2, Note 4.

16 For more detailed work on what can stay the same and what needs to change see Conceptual Framework for Sustainability Reporting – Capitals Coalition, especially the Appendix.

17 There is a lot of practice as well as standards on how to go about this for example SVI, UNDP and Capitals Coalition.

18 International Auditing and Assurance Standards Board. Extended External Reporting (EER) Assurance. IAASB, www.iaasb.org/consultations-projects/extended-external-reporting-eer-assurance (Accessed 15 April 2025.)

19 European Union. Directive (EU) 2024/1760 of the European Parliament and of the Council of 13 June 2024 on corporate sustainability due diligence and amending Directive (EU) 2019/1937 and Regulation (EU) 2023/2859. Official Journal of the European Union, L 2024/1760, 5 July 2024.

Chapter 10: How are we going to change it?

[1] www.ifrs.org/content/dam/ifrs/supporting-implementation/documents/effects-of-climate-related-matters-on-financial-statements.pdf (Accessed 14 August 2025.)

[2] www.ifrs.org/news-and-events/news/2024/07/iasb-improve-reporting-climate-related-other-uncertainties-fs/ (Accessed 6 February 2025.)

[3] See Chapter 8, Note 43.

[4] www.dirittobancario.it/wp-content/uploads/2025/07/Rapporto-EIOPA-30-giugno-2025-EIOPA-BoS-25-251.pdf (Accessed 4 August 2025.)

[5] https://tnfd.global/wp-content/uploads/2023/12/BNEF_Case-Studies_-Nature_Risk_When-bees-sting.pdf (Accessed 14 August 2025.)

[6] www.xrb.govt.nz/standards/accounting-standards/for-profit-standards/standards-list/nz-ias-1/ paragraph 17. (Accessed 30 August 2025.)

[7] www.datocms-assets.com/120585/1741658016-ffd4-negotiation-roadmap.pdf (Accessed 30 August 2025.)

[8] www.frc.org.uk/library/standards-codes-policy/accounting-and-reporting/true-and-fair-concept/ (Accessed 12 August 2025.)

[9] www.socialvalueint.org/s/True-and-Fair-signed-opinion (Accessed 12 August 2025.)

[10] https://friendsprovidentfoundation.org/grants/ (Accessed 5 February 2025.)

[11] www.oxfam.org/en/research/inequality-inc (Accessed 5 February 2025.)

Bibliography

Accountancy Europe. Definition of Public Interest Entities in Europe: State of Play After the Implementation of the 2014 Audit Reform. November 2017.

Accounting Standards Board. Statement of Principles for Financial Reporting. Accounting Standards Board, 1999.

Adnan, Muhammad Akhyar, and Nur Barizah Abu Bakar. 'Accounting Treatment for Corporate Zakat: A Critical Review.' *International Journal of Islamic and Middle Eastern Finance and Management*, vol. 2, no. 1, 2009, pp. 32–45.

Advisory Opinion AO-32/25 on Climate Emergency and Human Rights, Inter-American Court of Human Rights, adopted 29 May 2025, San José, Costa Rica.

Aho, James A. *Confession and Bookkeeping: The Religious, Moral, and Rhetorical Roots of Modern Accounting*. State University of New York Press, 2005.

Akala. *Natives: Race and Class in the Ruins of Empire*. John Murray, 2018.

Alborn, Timothy L. *Conceiving Companies: Joint-Stock Politics and Corporate Social Responsibility in Victorian England*. Routledge, 1998.

American Institute of Certified Public Accountants (AICPA). Statement on Standards for Attestation Engagements No. 20: Amendments to the Description of the Concept of Materiality. Auditing Standards Board, Dec. 2019.

American Institute of Certified Public Accountants. Study Group on the Objectives of Financial Statements. Objectives of Financial

Statements: Report of the Study Group on the Objectives of Financial Statements. American Institute of Certified Public Accountants, 1973.

Annisette, Marcia. 'Imperialism and the Professions: The Education and Certification of Accountants in Trinidad and Tobago.' *Accounting, Organizations and Society*, vol. 25, no. 7, 2000, pp. 631–659.

Annisette, Marcia and David Neu. 'Accounting and Empire: An Introduction.' *Critical Perspectives on Accounting*, vol. 15, no. 1, January 2004, pp. 1–4.

Anstey, Roger and P. E. H. Hair, editors. *Liverpool, the African Slave Trade, and Abolition: Essays to Illustrate Current Knowledge and Research*. Historic Society of Lancashire and Cheshire, 1976.

Baladouni, Vahe. 'Financial Reporting in the Early Years of the East India Company.' *Accounting Historians Journal*, vol. 13, no. 1, Spring 1986.

Baydoun, Nabil, and Roger Willett. 'Islamic Corporate Reports.' *Abacus*, vol. 36, no. 1, 2000.

Botzem, Sebastian. *The Politics of Accounting Regulation: Organizing Transnational Standard Setting in Financial Reporting*. Edward Elgar Publishing, 2012.

Boys, Peter. 'The Mystery of the Missing Members: The First 600 Chartered Accountants in England and Wales.' *Accounting, Business & Financial History*, vol. 14, no. 1, 2004.

Bregman, Rutger. *Humankind: A Hopeful History*. Translated by Elizabeth Manton and Erica Moore. Little, Brown and Company, 2020.

Breytenbach, S., and J. Nicholls. *Accounting for Impact: Financial and Sustainability Reporting of Relocating Graves in South Africa*. Capitals Coalition, 2024.

Briggs, Chris. 'Women, Legal Status and Market Participation in Late Medieval England: Some Thoughts on Recent Research / Mujeres, Estatus Legal y Participación en el Mercado en la Inglaterra Bajomedieval: Algunas Reflexiones Sobre Investigaciones Recientes.' *Cuadernos Medievales,* no. 35, December 2023, pp. 228–248. Grupo de Investigación y Estudios Medievales, Facultad de Humanidades – UNMdP, República Argentina. ISSN 2451-6821.

Broadbent, Jane. 'The Gendered Nature of "Accounting Logic": Pointers to an Accounting That Encompasses Multiple Values.' *Critical Perspectives on Accounting*, vol. 9, no. 3, 1998.

Brook, Peter, et al. 'Company Audits: Issues and Proposed Reforms.' House of Commons Library, 19 December 2023.

Brown, Christopher Leslie. *Moral Capital: Foundations of British Abolitionism*. University of North Carolina Press, 2006.

Burnard, Trevor and Giorgio Riello. 'Slavery and the New History of Capitalism.' *Journal of Global History*, vol. 15, no. 2, 2020.

Bush, Tim. Divided by Common Language: Where Economics Meets the Law—US Versus Non-US Financial Reporting Models. Institute of Chartered Accountants in England and Wales, June 2005. Reprinted November 2005.

Cairns, David. *The Conceptual Framework – the International Experience*. Working Paper, 22 June 2001.

Carchedi, Guglielmo and Michael Roberts. *Capitalism in the 21st Century: Through the Prism of Value*. Routledge, 2017.

Carnegie, Garry D., Delfina Gomes, Lee D. Parker, Karen McBride and Eva Tsahuridu. 'How Accounting Can Shape a Better World: Framework, Analysis and Research Agenda.' *Emerald Insight*, August 2024.

Cazel, Fred A., Jr. 'Financing the Crusades.' A History of the Crusades, edited by Kenneth M. Setton, vol. 6, *The Impact of the Crusades on Europe*, edited by Norman P. Zacour and Harry W. Hazard, University of Wisconsin Press, 1989.

Ceruzzi, Paul. *A History of Modern Computing.* MIT Press, 2000, p. 13.

Chambers, Robert. *Whose Reality Counts? Putting the First Last.* Intermediate Technology Publications, 1997.

Chancel, Lucas and Thomas Piketty. *Global Income Inequality, 1820–2020: The Persistence and Mutation of Extreme Inequality.* 2021, halshs-03321887.

Chenoweth, Erica and Zoe Marks. 'Revenge of the Patriarchs: Why Autocrats Fear Women.' *Foreign Affairs*, vol. 101, no. 2, March/April 2022.

Chiapello, Eve. 'Accounting and the Birth of the Notion of Capitalism.' *Critical Perspectives on Accounting*, vol. 18, no. 3, 2007.

Christov-Moore, Leonardo and Marco Iacoboni. 'Sex Differences in Somatomotor Representations of Others,' Pain: A Permutation-Based Analysis.' *Brain Structure and Function*, vol. 224, no. 2, March 2019.

Cooper, Christine. 'The Non and Nom of Accounting for (M)other Nature.' *Accounting, Auditing & Accountability Journal*, vol. 5, no. 3, 1992, pp. 16–39.

Cooper, David J. and Michael J. Sherer. 'The Value of Corporate Accounting Reports: Arguments for a Political Economy of Accounting.' *Accounting, Organizations and Society*, vol. 9, no. 3–4, 1984, pp. 207–232.

Cordery, Carolyn. 'Accounting History and Religion: A Review of Studies and a Research Agenda.' *Accounting History*, vol. 20, no. 4, 2015.

Criado Perez, Caroline. *Invisible Women: Data Bias in a World Designed for Men*. Abrams Press, 2019.

Cristea, Stefana, Delia David, and Luminița Păiușan. 'Specific Features of Islamic Accounting and Cultural Paradigm.' Munich Personal RePEc Archive, MPRA Paper No. 27174, 2010.

Darmawan, I Made Dwi Hita and I Gusti Ngurah Agung Panji Tresna. 'Accounting, Culture, and Hinduism: A Narrative Review.' Vidyottama Sanatana: *International Journal of Hindu Science and Religious Studies*, vol. 1, no. 2, 2017.

Davie, S. S. K. 'Accounting, Female and Male Gendering and Cultural Imperialism.' *Accounting, Auditing & Accountability Journal*, vol. 30, no. 2, 2017.

Davoudi, Leonardo, et al. 'The Historical Role of the Corporation in Society.' *Journal of the British Academy*, vol. 6, suppl. 1, 2018, pp. 17–47.

Diamond, Jared M. *Why Is Sex Fun? The Evolution of Human Sexuality*. 1st edn. HarperCollins, 1997.

Doll, Richard and A. Bradford Hill. 'Smoking and Carcinoma of the Lung: Preliminary Report.' *British Medical Journal*, vol. 2, no. 4682, 1950.

Doris, Glen. 'The Failure of Sympathy: Adam Smith's 'Moral Sentiments' and Slavery.' *Academia Letters*, Article 91, 2020.

Edelman Trust Institute. 2025 Edelman Trust Barometer: Global Report. Edelman, January 2025.

Epurescu-Pascovici, Ionuț (ed.). *Accounts and Accountability in Late Medieval Europe: Records, Procedures, and Socio-Political Impact. Utrecht Studies in Medieval Literacy*. Turnhout, Belgium: Brepols, 2020.

European Parliament and Council of the European Union. Directive (EU) 2022/2464 of 14 December 2022 Amending Regulation (EU) No 537/2014, Directive 2004/109/EC, Directive 2006/43/EC and Directive 2013/34/EU, as Regards Corporate Sustainability Reporting. Official Journal of the European Union, L 322/15, 16 Dec. 2022.

Federici, Silvia. *Caliban and the Witch: Women, the Body and Primitive Accumulation*. Autonomedia, 2004.

Federici, Silvia. *Re-enchanting the World: Feminism and the Politics of the Commons*. PM Press, 2018.

Federici, Silvia. *Witches, Witch-Hunting, and Women*. PM Press, 2018.

'Fiduciary Duty in the 21st Century.' Principles for Responsible Investment, 22 October 2019.

Financial Accounting Standards Board (FASB). Statement of Financial Accounting Concepts No. 8: Conceptual Framework for Financial Reporting—Chapter 7: Presentation. FASB, 2021, Retrieved from www.fasb.org/Page/ShowPdf?path=CON8-Ch7Presentation.pdf.

Financial Accounting Standards Board. Statement of Financial Accounting Concepts No. 8: Conceptual Framework for Financial Reporting. Financial Accounting Foundation, 2021.

Fine, Ben. *Social Capital versus Social Theory: Political Economy and Social Science at the Turn of the Millennium*. Routledge, 2001.

Fontaine, Laurence. *The Moral Economy: Poverty, Credit, and Trust in Early Modern Europe*. Cambridge University Press, 2014.

Foucault, Michel. *Power/Knowledge: Selected Interviews and Other Writings, 1972–1977*. Edited by Colin Gordon, Pantheon Books, 1980.

France. Law No. 2019-486 of May 22, 2019, on the Growth and Transformation of Companies. WIPO Lex, World Intellectual Property Organization, 2019.

French, Katherine L. *Household Goods and Good Households in Late Medieval London: Consumption and Domesticity After the Plague.* University of Pennsylvania Press, 2021.

Freshfields Bruckhaus Deringer. A Legal Framework for the Integration of Environmental, Social and Governance Issues into Institutional Investment. United Nations Environment Programme Finance Initiative, October 2005.

Froese, Tobias, et al. 'Degrowth-Oriented Organisational Value Creation: A Systematic Literature Review of Case Studies.' *Ecological Economics*, vol. 207, 2023, 107765.

'From Poverty to Punishment: Examining Laws and Practices Which Criminalise Women Due to Poverty or Status Worldwide. Penal Reform International and Women Beyond Walls', March 2025.

Gleeson-White, Jane. *Double Entry: How the Merchants of Venice Created Modern Finance.* W. W. Norton & Company, 2012.

Goddard, Richard. 'Female Merchants? Women, Debt, and Trade in Later Medieval England, 1266–1532.' *Journal of British Studies*, vol. 58, no. 3, July 2019.

Gramsci, Antonio. *Selections from the Prison Notebooks.* Edited and translated by Quintin Hoare and Geoffrey Nowell Smith, International Publishers, 1971.

Haggerty, Sheryllynne. 'The Structure of the Trading Community in Liverpool, 1760–1810.' *Transactions of the Historic Society of Lancashire and Cheshire*, vol. 151, 2002.

Harper, Alfred, compiler. *The Accountants' Directory for 1877.* Williams & Strahan, 1876.

Hanke, Lewis. 'Pope Paul III and the American Indians.' *Harvard Theological Review*, vol. 30, no. 2, April 1937.

Heblich, Stephan, et al. 'Slavery and the British Industrial Revolution.' CAGE Online Working Paper Series, no. 656, 2023, Centre for Competitive Advantage in the Global Economy (CAGE), University of Warwick.

Hickel, Jason, et al. 'A Fair-Shares Assessment of Resource Use, 1970–2017.' *The Lancet Planetary Health*, vol. 6, no. 7, 2022.

Hill, Jennifer G. 'Shifting Contours of Directors' Fiduciary Duties and Norms in Comparative Corporate Governance.' ECGI Law Working Paper, no. 489/2020, January 2020.

Hines, Ruth D. 'Financial Accounting: In Communicating Reality, We Construct Reality.' *Accounting, Organizations and Society*, vol. 13, no. 3, 1988.

Hirschman, Albert O. *Exit, Voice, and Loyalty: Responses to Decline in Firms, Organizations, and States*. Harvard University Press, 1970.

Hoogervorst, Hans. 'Working in the Public Interest: The IFRS Foundation and the IASB.' IFRS Foundation, 8 April 2016.

Hopwood, Anthony G. and Peter Miller, editors. *Accounting as Social and Institutional Practice*. Cambridge Studies in Management, Cambridge University Press, 1994.

Hunter, Tera W. *Bound in Wedlock: Slave and Free Black Marriage in the Nineteenth Century*. Harvard University Press, 2017.

Hurth, Victoria, Ben Renshaw and Lorenzo Fioramonti. *Beyond Profit: Purpose-Driven Leadership for a Well-being Economy*. John Murray Business, 2025.

ICAEW, *Accounting Standards 1977*, ICAEW, 1977.

ICAEW. Acting in the Public Interest: A Framework for Analysis. Institute of Chartered Accountants in England and Wales, 2012.

ICAEW. *Shaping Sustainability Standard Setting: What Lessons Can Sustainability Standard-Setters Learn from the Experience of Accounting Standard-Setters?* 2024.

IFRS Foundation. *Due Process Handbook*. August 2020. IFRS Foundation.

Inikori, Joseph E. 'Slavery and Atlantic Commerce, 1650–1800.' *The American Economic Review*, vol. 82, no. 2, May 1992.

International Accounting Standards Board. *Conceptual Framework for Financial Reporting*. IFRS Foundation, March 2018.

International Accounting Standards Board. *Definition of Material (Amendments to IAS 1 and IAS 8)*. IFRS Foundation, October 2018.

International Accounting Standards Board. *Discount Rates in IFRS Standards: Project Summary*. IFRS Foundation, February 2019.

International Accounting Standards Committee. *Framework for the Preparation and Presentation of Financial Statements*. IASC, 1989.

International Court of Justice. *Obligations of States in Respect of Climate Change: Advisory Opinion*. International Court of Justice, 23 July 2025.

International Federation of Accountants. *Policy Position 5: A Definition of the Public Interest*. June 2012.

International Financial Reporting Standards Foundation. *IFRS Foundation Constitution*. November 2021.

International Financial Reporting Standards Foundation. *Effects of Climate-Related Matters on Financial Statements*. Republished July 2023

International Integrated Reporting Council. International <IR> Framework, January 2021.

International Labour Organization. *Wage Policies, Including Living Wages: Report for Discussion at the Meeting of Experts on Wage Policies, Including Living Wages* (Geneva, 19–23 February 2024). International Labour Office, 2023.

International Organization of Securities Commissions. *Objectives and Principles of Securities Regulation*. May 2017.

International Public Sector Accounting Standards Board (IPSASB). *Conceptual Framework for General Purpose Financial Reporting by Public Sector Entities*. December 2023.

International Public Sector Accounting Standards Board (IPSASB). *Recommended Practice Guideline (RPG) 3: Reporting Service Performance Information*. International Federation of Accountants, April 2015.

International Public Sector Accounting Standards Board. *The Conceptual Framework for General Purpose Financial Reporting by Public Sector Entities*. International Federation of Accountants (IFAC), October 2014.

Ives, Kelly. *Cixous, Irigaray, Kristeva. The Jouissance of French Feminism*. Crescent Moon Publishing, 1998.

Jackson, Tim. *Prosperity Without Growth: Foundations for the Economy of Tomorrow*. 2nd ed., Routledge, 2017.

Jackson, Tim. 'The False Economy of Big Food and the Case for a New Food Economy.' Food, Farming and Countryside Commission, 2024.

James, Selma. *Our Time Is Now: Sex, Race, Class, and Caring for People and Planet*. PM Press, 2021.

Janega, Eleanor. *The Once and Future Sex: Going Medieval on Women's Roles in Society*. Paperback edn, Icon Books, 2024.

Jones, Phil. *Work Without the Worker: Labour in the Age of Platform Capitalism*. Verso, 2021.

Kamla, Rania, and Faizul Haque. 'Islamic Accounting, Neo-Imperialism and Identity Staging: The Accounting and Auditing Organization for Islamic Financial Institutions.' *Critical Perspectives on Accounting*, vol. 63, 2019, article 102097.

Kamla, Rania. 'Critically Appreciating Social Accounting and Reporting in the Arab Middle East: A Postcolonial Perspective.' *Advances in International Accounting*, vol. 20, 2007.

Keller, A. Craig, Katherine T. Smith and L. Murphy Smith. 'Do Gender, Educational Level, Religiosity, and Work Experience Affect the Ethical Decision-Making of U.S. Accountants?' *Accounting Education*, vol. 16, no. 1, 2007.

Kelly, Marjorie. *Wealth Supremacy: How the Extractive Economy and the Biased Rules of Capitalism Drive Today's Crises*. Berrett-Koehler Publishers, 2023.

King, Thomas A. *More Than a Numbers Game: A Brief History of Accounting*. John Wiley & Sons, 2006.

Kirsch, Robert J. *The International Accounting Standards Committee: A Political History*. Wolters Kluwer (UK) Limited, 2006.

Komori, Naoko. 'Towards the Feminization of Accounting Practice: Lessons from the Experiences of Japanese Women in the Accounting Profession.' *Accounting, Auditing & Accountability Journal*, vol. 21, no. 4, 2008, pp. 507–538.

Lamont, Michèle, and Marcel Fournier, editors. *Cultivating Differences: Symbolic Boundaries and the Making of Inequality*. University of Chicago Press, 1992.

Lee, Stewart. 'Stewart Lee: Content Provider (2018) – Transcript.' Scraps from the Loft, 10 February 2020.

Lester, V. Markham. 'Some Characteristics of Insolvency Levels.' *Victorian Insolvency: Bankruptcy, Imprisonment for Debt, and Company Winding-Up in Nineteenth-Century England.* Oxford University Press, 1995.

Levy, Jonathan. 'Accounting for Profit and the History of Capital.' *Critical Historical Studies*, vol. 1, no. 2, Fall 2014.

Lindert, Peter H., and Jeffrey G. Williamson. 'American Colonial Incomes, 1650–1774.' NBER Working Paper, no. 19861, January 2014. National Bureau of Economic Research.

Lynn, Martin. 'Trade and Politics in 19th-Century Liverpool: The Tobin and Horsfall Families and Liverpool's African Trade.' *Transactions of the Historic Society of Lancashire and Cheshire*, vol. 142, 1992.

Maher, Stephen and Scott M. Aquanno. *The Fall and Rise of American Finance: From J.P. Morgan to BlackRock.* Verso, 13 February 2024.

Mair, John. *Book-keeping Methodiz'd: Or, a Methodical Treatise of Merchant-Accompts, According to the Italian Form.* 2nd edn, with additions and improvements, London, 1741.

Malaysian Accounting Standards Board. *Technical Release i-1: Accounting for Zakat on Business.* 2006.

Mandle, Jon, and David Schmidtz, editors. *The Oxford Handbook of Ethics and Economics.* Oxford University Press, 2019.

Manjapra, Kris. *The Black Ghost of Empire: The Long Death of Slavery and the Failure of Emancipation.* Scribner, 2022.

Marcacci, Antonio. *Transnational Securities Regulation: How It Works, Who Shapes It.* Springer, 2022.

Marx, Karl. *Capital: A Critique of Political Economy*. Translated by Samuel Moore and Edward Aveling, edited by Friedrich Engels, vol. 1, C.H. Kerr & Company, 1887.

Mayson, Stephen. *Legal Services Regulation: The Meaning of 'The Public Interest'*. Centre for Ethics and Law, University College London, 2024.

May, Channing. 'Transnational Crime and the Developing World.' *Global Financial Integrity*, March 2017.

Mazzucato, Mariana. *The Value of Everything: Making and Taking in the Global Economy*. PublicAffairs, 2018.

McGlaughlin, Mary and Bonnnie Wheeler. *The Letters of Heloise and Abelard*. Palgrave Macmillan, 2009.

McNicholas, Patty. 'Maori Feminism: A Contribution to Accounting Research and Practice.' Paper presented at the Fourth Asia Pacific Interdisciplinary Research in Accounting Conference, 4–6 July 2004, Singapore.

Meltzer, Milton. *Slavery: A World History*. 1st Da Capo Press edn, Da Capo Press, 1993.

Merseyside Maritime Museum. *Archives of William Davenport (1725–1797)*. Reference Code: D/DAV, Accession No.: MMM.2002.64. National Museums Liverpool, UK.

Mies, Maria. *Patriarchy and Accumulation on a World Scale: Women in the International Division of Labour*. Zed Books, 1986.

Milanovic, Branko. 'Changes in the Global Income Distribution and Their Political Consequences.' *Survival*, vol. 61, no. 2, 2019.

Miley, Frances Myfanwy and Andrew Farley Read. 'Accounting Lessons from a Medieval Woman: The Writing of Christine de Pisan.' European Accounting Association 39th Annual Congress, Maastricht, the Netherlands, May 2016.

Monitoring Group. Public Interest Framework for the Development of International Audit-Related Standards. 2020.

Murtin, Fabrice, and Vincent Siegerink. Valuing Business Impacts in the Areas of Wage Inequality and Employee Well-being. OECD Papers on Well-being and Inequalities, no. 15, OECD Publishing, 2023.

Neimark, Marilyn Kleinberg. 'Regicide Revisited: Marx, Foucault and Accounting.' *Critical Perspectives on Accounting*, vol. 5, no. 1, 1994.

New Zealand Accounting Standards Board. Public Benefit Entity Financial Reporting Standard 48: Service Performance Reporting (PBE FRS 48). Issued November 2017, incorporating amendments to 31 August 2020.

Nicholls, Jeremy, and Thaddeus Zochowski. *Mutually Compatible, Yet Different: A Theoretical Framework for Reconciling Different Impact Monetization Methodologies and Frameworks*. SSRN, 20 October 2020.

Nicholls, Jeremy. *A Framework for Successful Sustainability Standard Setting*. ICAEW, 2024.

Nobes, Christopher and Robert Parker. *Comparative International Accounting*. 13th edn, Pearson, 2020.

OECD. *Global Debt Report 2025: Financing Growth in a Challenging Debt Market Environment*. OECD Publishing, 2025.

OECD. *The Polluter Pays Principle: Definition, Analysis, Implementation*, OECD Publishing, 2008.

Our World in Data. (2023). *Global GDP over the long run*.

Paine, Thomas. *Rights of Man*. Joseph Johnson and J.S. Jordan, 1791.

Palpacuer, Florence and Alistair Smith, editors. *Rethinking Value Chains: Tackling the Challenges of Global Capitalism*. Springer, 2021.

Parliament of the World's Religions. 'Towards a Global Ethic: An Initial Declaration'. 2020 update, Parliament of the World's Religions, 2023.

Parvez Butt, Anam, et al. 'Radical Pathways Beyond GDP: Why and How We Need to Pursue Feminist and Decolonial Alternatives Urgently'. Oxfam GB, 3 August 2023.

Peterson, Gayle, Robert Yawson, Ellen J. K. and Jeremy Nicholls. *Navigating Big Finance and Big Technology for Global Change*. Palgrave Macmillan, 2020.

Piketty, Thomas. *A Brief History of Equality*. Translated by Steven Rendall. Belknap Press of Harvard University Press, 2022.

Policy Exchange. 'Who Should Decide Who Decides the Public Interest?' Policy Exchange, 16 February 2016.

Poullaos, Chris and Sian, Suki. *Accountancy and Empire: The British Legacy of Professional Organization*. Routledge, 2004.

Ramos, Jennifer and Zaneta Sedilekova. *Biodiversity Risk: Legal Implications for Companies and Their Directors*. Commonwealth Climate and Law Initiative, 13 December 2022, corrected May 2023.

Ramstad, Yngve. 'John R. Commons's Reasonable Value and the Problem of Just Price.' *Journal of Economic Issues*, vol. 35, no. 2, June 2001.

Reynaud, Emmanuel. 'The International Labour Organization and the Living Wage: A Historical Perspective'. *International Labour Organization*, 2017.

Riccaboni, Angelo, Elena Giovannoni, Andrea Giorgi and Stefano Moscadelli. 'Accounting and Power: Evidence from the Fourteenth Century.' *Accounting History*, vol. 11, no. 1, 2006.

Robins, Jonathan E. *Oil Palm: A Global History*. University of North Carolina Press, 2021.

Rönnbäck, Klas. 'On the Economic Importance of the Slave Plantation Complex to the British Economy during the Eighteenth Century: A Value-Added Approach.' *Journal of Global History*, vol. 13, no. 3, 2018.

Rose, Amanda M. 'The "Reasonable Investor" of Federal Securities Law: Insights from Tort Law's "Reasonable Person" & Suggested Reforms.' *The Journal of Corporation Law*, vol. 43, no. 1, 2017.

Rosenthal, Caitlin. *Accounting for Slavery: Masters and Management*. Harvard University Press, 2018.

Roser, Max, et al. *'World GDP over the Last Two Millennia.'* Our World in Data, 2017, https://ourworldindata.org/economic-growth. Adapted under CC BY 4.0.

Roy, Arundhati. *Capitalism: A Ghost Story*. Haymarket Books, 2014.

Ruggie, John. Protect, Respect and Remedy: A Framework for Business and Human Rights. Report of the Special Representative of the Secretary-General on the Issue of Human Rights and Transnational Corporations and Other Business Enterprises, United Nations Human Rights Council, 7 April 2008.

S&P Global Sustainable1. Unpriced Environmental Costs: The Top Externalities of the Global Market. Prepared in collaboration with Capitals Coalition, August 2024.

Saad, Aisha I. and Diane Strauss. 'The New "Reasonable Investor" and Changing Frontiers of Materiality: Increasing Investor Reliance on ESG Disclosures and Implications for Securities Litigation.' *Berkeley Business Law Journal*, vol. 17, no. 2, 2020.

Sahan, Erinch, et al. *What Doughnut Economics Means for Business: Creating Enterprises That Are Regenerative and Distributive by Design*. Doughnut Economics Action Lab, November 2022.

Saini, Angela. *The Patriarchs: The Origins of Inequality*. HarperCollins, 2023.

Sales, Lord. 'The Interface between Contract and Equity.' Lehane Memorial Lecture, 28 August 2019, Sydney. Supreme Court of the United Kingdom.

Salman, Kautsar Riza. 'Exploring the History of Islamic Accounting and the Concept of Accountability in an Islamic Perspective.' *Journal of Islamic Economic and Business Research*, vol. 2, no. 2, December 2022.

Sánchez-Bayo, Francisco and Kris A.G. Wyckhuys. 'Worldwide Decline of the Entomofauna: A Review of Its Drivers.' *Biological Conservation*, vol. 232, April 2019.

Sandström, Anders. *Anarchist Accounting: Theory and Practice.* International Organisation for a Participatory Society, 2011.

Sangster, Alan, et al. 'The Determination of Profit in Medieval Times.' *Information Technology Science.* Edited by Valentina Dagienė and Ida N. F. Specht, vol. 715, Advances in Intelligent Systems and Computing, Springer, 2018.

Schumpeter, Joseph A. *The Theory of Economic Development: An Inquiry into Profits, Capital, Credit, Interest and the Business Cycle.* 1934. Transaction Publishers, 2008.

Seldon, John. *Table-talk, Being Discourses of John Seldon, Esq or His Sense of Various Matters of Weight and High Consequence, Relating Especially to Religion and State.* Jacob Tonson et al, 1696, p. 54. https://quod.lib.umich.edu/e/eebo/A59095.0001.001/1:40?rgn=div1;view=fulltext&utm (Accessed 7 October 2025.)

Senkl, Daniela, and Christine Cooper. 'On Valuing (M)other Nature in Times of Climate Crises: A Reflection on the Non and Nom of Accounting for (M)other Nature.' *Critical Perspectives on Accounting*, vol. 91, 2023.

Shanin, Teodor, editor. *Peasants and Peasant Societies.* 2nd edn, Blackwell, 1987.

Shepard, Alexandra, and Tim Stretton. 'Women Negotiating the Boundaries of Justice in Britain, 1300–1700: An Introduction.' *Journal of British Studies*, vol. 58, no. 4, October 2019.

Shutt, Harry. *Beyond the Profits System: Possibilities for a Post-Capitalist Era*. Zed Books, 2010.

Sikka, Prem. 'The Hand of Accounting and Accountancy Firms in Deepening Income and Wealth Inequalities and the Economic Crisis: Some Evidence.' *Critical Perspectives on Accounting*, vol. 30, July 2015.

Smith, Adam. *An Inquiry into the Nature and Causes of the Wealth of Nations*. Edited by Edwin Cannan, Modern Library, 1994.

Smith, Adam. *The Theory of Moral Sentiments. 1759*. Edited by Knud Haakonssen, Cambridge University Press, 2002.

Soll, Jacob. *The Reckoning: Financial Accountability and the Rise and Fall of Nations*. Basic Books, 2014.

Stiglitz, Joseph E. *The Great Divide: Unequal Societies and What We Can Do About Them*. W.W. Norton & Company, 2015.

Stiglitz, Joseph E. *The Price of Inequality: How Today's Divided Society Endangers Our Future*. W.W. Norton & Company, 2012.

Stiglitz, Joseph E. *The Road to Freedom*. Allen Lane, 2024.

Svanberg, Marja K. and Carl F. C. Svanberg. 'Is There Such a Thing as a Good Profit? Taking Conventional Ethics Seriously.' *Philosophia*, vol. 49, 2021.

'The Problems, Progress, and Potential of Performance Reporting.' Office of the Auditor-General New Zealand, 2021.

Tinker, Tony. *Paper Prophets: A Social Critique of Accounting*. Holt, Rinehart and Winston, 1985.

Toms, Steven. 'Double Entry and the Rise of Capitalism: Keeping a Sense of Proportion?' *Accounting History Review*, vol. 26, no. 1, 2016.

Trust, Sandy, et al. 'The Emperor's New Climate Scenarios: Limitations and Assumptions of Commonly Used Climate-Change Scenarios in Financial Services.' Institute and Faculty of Actuaries, 4 July 2023.

Tsuji, Atsuo, and Paul Garner, editors. *Studies in Accounting History: Japan, the West and Beyond.* Routledge, 2008.

Tuovila, Alicia. 'Mark to Market (MTM): What It Means in Accounting, Finance, and Investing.' Investopedia, updated 17 November 2023.

Turkish Republic Ministry of Finance, Strategy Development Unit. *Accounting Method Used by Ottomans for 500 Years: Stairs (Merdiban) Method.*

Tweedie, David, Allan Cook and Geoffrey Whittington. *The UK Accounting Standards Board, 1990–2000: Restoring Honesty and Trust in Accounting.* Routledge, 2024.

United Nations Development Programme. *SDG Impact Standards for Enterprises.* UNDP, 2021. https://sdgimpact.undp.org/sdg-impact-standards/standards-for-enterprises.html

United Nations Environment Programme Finance Initiative, et al. Fiduciary Duty in the 21st Century. UNEP FI, 2015.

United Nations Office on Drugs and Crime. World Drug Report 2024. United Nations, 2024.

Ville, Simon, and Grant Fleming. 'Desperately Seeking Synergy: Interdisciplinary Research in Accounting and Business History.' *Pacific Accounting Review*, vol. 11, no. 1/2, 1999.

Widmann, Johannes. Behende und hüpsche Rechenung auff allen Kauffmanschafft. Leipzig, 1489.

World Economic Forum. *Global Gender Gap Report 2023*. Geneva: World Economic Forum, 2023.

Wright, Jeremy. 'The Attorney General on Who Should Decide What the Public Interest Is.' GOV.UK, 8 Feb. 2016.

Young, Joni J. 'Making Up Users.' *Accounting, Organizations and Society*, vol. 31, no. 6, 2006.

'What Does Your Job Say About You?' *The Times*, October 2024.

You, Leyuan, et al. 'An Empirical Study of Multiple Direct International Listings.' *Global Finance Journal*, vol. 24, no. 1, 2013.

Zola, Émile. *Germinal*. Translated by Leonard Tancock, Penguin Classics, 1954.

Acknowledgements

I have been humbled by the amount of time and effort everyone I asked was willing to contribute to making this a better book, providing help with technical knowledge, editing and ideas.

Mario Abela, Ben Carpenter, Bonnie Chiu, Nick Drape, Eddie Finch, Fabienne Michaux, Jenni Ramos, Ainurul Rosli, Jenni Rose, Marje Russ, Neal Umney, Lucinda Riding, Delilah Rothenberg, Helen Slinger, Emma Smith – thank you.

The team at Practical Inspiration have been brilliant, from the first meeting with Alison, to being guided through the process of writing, structuring and editing (down). And keeping me to a timetable!

And thank you all for stopping me starting sentences with 'and'. Mostly.

This book would never have happened without Richard Pearce. He was my tutor at Reading University when I was studying Agricultural Economics. I arrived as non-thinking non-critical undergraduate and left knowing that I would be working on inequality. Since then, I tried to get back in contact with Richard but without success. I discovered too late, only on reading his obituary, that he had left economics to become a psychotherapist. His practice was called the Quiet Space, chosen to 'highlight the place within us we often seek to find, and which, through the turbulence and sometimes anguish of living our lives we lose or fail to discover'. My one regret is that I was not able to find him and say thank you.

I can, though, thank Sara Williams. The nature of writing a book means that there is an author, the person who writes and is responsible. But writing is also a creative process and many of the ideas in this book, the linkages and the connections between accounting and the world we live in, come from the discussions that Sara and I had as we walked up and down a lot of hills, mainly in Wales and Andalucia.

We didn't *just* talk about accounting; we talked about politics, economics, culture, history, gender, power and accountability, but the connections kept springing up. This would be a much thinner and less interesting book if it hadn't been for Sara's thinking. And a far less readable one had it not been for her repeated and extensive editing.

Index

Note: page numbers in *italic* type refer to figures; those in **bold** type refer to tables.

A quick word from Practical Inspiration Publishing...

We hope you found this book both practical and inspiring – that's what we aim for with every book we publish.

We publish titles on topics ranging from leadership, entrepreneurship, HR and marketing to self-development and wellbeing.

Find details of all our books at: www.practicalinspiration.com

Did you know...

We can offer discounts on bulk sales of all our titles – ideal if you want to use them for training purposes, corporate giveaways or simply because you feel these ideas deserve to be shared with your network.

We can even produce bespoke versions of our books, for example with your organization's logo and/or a tailored foreword.

To discuss further, contact us on info@practicalinspiration.com.

Got an idea for a business book?

We may be able to help. Find out about more about publishing in partnership with us at: bit.ly/PIpublishing.

Follow us on social media...

 @PIPTalking

 @pip_talking

 @practicalinspiration

 @piptalking

 Practical Inspiration Publishing

www.ingramcontent.com/pod-product-compliance
Lightning Source LLC
Chambersburg PA
CBHW021920190326
41519CB00009B/866

* 9 7 8 1 7 8 8 6 0 7 1 3 1 *